MEXICO DURING THE WAR WITH THE UNITED STATES

Mexico During the War with the United States

BY JOSÉ FERNANDO RAMÍREZ

Edited by
Walter V. Scholes
Translated by
Elliott B. Scherr

University of Missouri Press
Columbia

SBN 8262-0594-1
Library of Congress Catalog Card Number A51-9129
Manufactured in the United States of America
Originally printed by the University of Missouri
as Volume XXIII, Number 1
of the University of Missouri Studies, 1950
Reprinted 1970 by the University of Missouri Press
Columbia, Missouri 65201

CONTENTS

PREFACE

This translation of José Fernando Ramírez's "México durante su guerra con los Estados Unidos" is made from Volume III of Genaro García's *Documentos inéditos o muy raros para la historia de México* (Mexico City, 1905). Chapter headings and footnotes (unless otherwise indicated) are by the present editor. One letter in the García edition has been omitted because it had little to do with Mexico during the war period. The undersigned are indebted to Sr. Lic. Trinidad García of Mexico City for permission to print this translation of his father's work.

W. V. S.
E. B. S.

INTRODUCTION

It is surprising that José Fernando Ramírez, both politically and intellectually an outstanding figure in nineteenth-century Mexico, has yet to attract a biographer worthy of his stature. Born in the frontier province of Chihuahua in 1805, Ramírez was educated in Durango, Guadalajara, and Mexico City. Although he received a law degree in 1832, he did not concentrate on his profession, for his wide-ranging interests drew him into politics, history, archaeology, and literature. As early as 1846 the Sociedad de Geografía y Estadística of Mexico, recognizing the breadth of his scholarship, made him a member of that organization.

Although involved in Mexican politics, Ramírez always seemed to find time to pursue his personal interests. In 1852 he became the Director of the National Museum. On a tour abroad in 1855-1856, he studied Mexican codices that had found their way into European collections, and the experience convinced him that in the future Mexican manuscripts must be preserved in Mexico. Despite his efforts, however, he met with little success in getting such a policy adopted. Based on his research, he published *Notas y esclarecimientos a la historia de la Conquista de México del Sr. W. Prescott, Noticias de la vida y escritos de Fray Toribio de Benavente o Motolinia,* and various articles on Indian civilizations in pre-Conquest Mexico. His most famous works, *Apuntes para la historia del Imperio de Maximiliano* and the work herein translated were published after he died.

Ramírez's *México durante su guerra con los Estados Unidos* is important because it describes so vividly the chaotic conditions that prevailed just before and during the war. Since most books published in the United States pay little attention to internal Mexican affairs, Ramírez's work should help Americans understand Mexico in the mid-1840's.

At the time of the war, Mexico had been independent for a quarter of a century, years in which liberals and conservatives had constantly struggled for power. Many opportunists—Santa Anna is probably the most noteworthy example—were able to take advantage of the turmoil and to rule as pseudo-dictators. Although in retrospect one can see that the liberals were gradually gaining the advantage, the full effect of the liberal movement would not become apparent until the 1850's and 1860's. However, in late 1844 the liberals, back in control, forced Santa Anna into exile and put José Joaquín Herrera into the presidency. But Herrera's middle-of-the-road leadership satisfied few Mexicans, and, as a result, in December 1845 the conservatives took their turn at revolution under the leadership of General Mariano Paredes and General Gabriel Valencia. Although the new junta succeeded in ousting Herrera, it could not agree on his successor, many of the leaders even favoring Santa Anna's recall. On the verge of war with the United States, Mexico was at the same time experiencing another domestic upheaval.

The Mexicans believed at the time that the United States alone was responsible for the outbreak of the war in 1846, and they have never changed their opinion. (They disagree among themselves over why the war was lost.) Americans find various causes for the war: constant revolutions, which led to nonpayment of American claims, Mexico's inability to effectively control the California-New Mexico frontier area, the sense of Anglo-Saxon superiority that justified expansion at the expense of lesser races, the need to enlarge the American agricultural frontier, the desire to facilitate trade in the Pacific by acquiring ports in California. Within this framework, some authors even charge President Polk with deliberately plotting the war. According to the uninhibited nineteenth-century American writer Hubert Howe Bancroft: "It was a premeditated and predetermined affair, the war of the United States on Mexico; it was the result of a deliberately calculated scheme of robbery on the part of the superior power." While arguments persist on the causes of the war, there is general agreement that the United States was determined never to relinquish the newly annexed territory of Texas and somehow to acquire California.

After the United States had annexed Texas, Mexico broke off diplomatic relations and both sides made tentative preparations for war. In addition, Polk sent William S. Parrott to Mexico City as his confidential agent to see if the Mexicans would be willing to discuss the outstanding issues between the two nations. When Parrott reported his conviction that Mexico would receive an American envoy—a belief confirmed by the Mexican Minister of Foreign Affairs in October 1845 — Polk appointed John Slidell as Envoy Extraordinary and Minister Plenipotentiary with full powers to discuss claims, California, and the Texas boundary. Specifically, Slidell's objectives were to establish the Rio Grande River as the American-Mexican boundary, to buy New Mexico for $5,000,000 if possible, and to pay as high as $25,000,000 for California. In return the United States would agree to assume the claims of its citizens against the Mexican Government.

Because accepting an envoy with Slidell's credentials would automatically have restored diplomatic relations with the United States, the Mexican Government refused to receive Slidell when he presented himself in Mexico City. Mexico had severed relations with the United States and was not about to renew them simply through a procedural technicality. In 1877, when Mexico was anxious for American recognition and tried a similar stratagem, the Americans too refused to be taken in. Slidell's mission having failed, the United States and Mexico unfortunately found no way to settle their differences. In May 1846 the United States issued a formal declaration of war.

Ramírez's text begins in December 1845.

W. V. S.

May, 1970
Columbia, Missouri

CHAPTER I

THE FALL OF HERRERA

El Siglo XIX[1] has published the following article:

"Several letters reaching us yesterday through the mails inform us that in that city [in San Luis][2] a considerable quantity of military baggage has been seized and that the infantry is beginning to leave for this capital. God save the nation in this sad and difficult period when so many have it within their power to hasten the Republic on the road to anarchy!" For more than a month now we have been living in the most distressing uncertainty as the result of such information as the foregoing. This information was considered authentic, since it consisted of letters written by officers of General Paredes's army itself. The President[3] saw them but he did not believe them, or else his Cabinet lacked the energy necessary to give them credence. The fact is that the *Diario*[4] wrote several articles eulogizing Paredes, believing that thereby it was disarming him. When it was positively ascertained that his cavalry was in San Miguel and Celaya[5] the Minister of War[6] kept calm, telling me that *they had come to guard the roads during the holidays and to save the expenses of fodder, which was costly in San Luis.* I have never before seen so much mental inertia and incapacity gathered together in one cabinet. Don Luis Cuevas[7] has been unperturbed and confident during the past few days. Pedraza[8] seemed nervous and undecided.

Valencia[9] went to his estate with his entire family on the seventeenth. I believe that he is unreliable.

It is generally thought that Pedraza is the soul of the Cabinet, and as such he is being harassed by the press with unexampled fury. I do not, however, believe that he is anything of the sort, and I am of the opinion that he has done the most stupid thing that a man in public life can do, for he has been taking less and less part in the Government, thinking thus to still the outcries against him. But he has not foreseen the fact that his enemies

1 *The Nineteenth Century.* This was one of Mexico's outstanding liberal newspapers.
2 A city northwest of Mexico City in the state of San Luis Potosí.
3 Herrera. For a more favorable view of Herrera than that presented by Ramírez see Thomas E. Cotner's *The Military and Political Career of José Joaquín de Herrera, 1792-1854* (Austin, 1949).
4 *Diario Oficial.* The official publication of the Mexican Government.
5 Both of these towns are in the state of Guanajuato, which is south of San Luis Potosí.
6 Pedro María Anaya, who later became acting President, April-May, 1847.
7 Luis Cuevas was a conservative who had served as Minister of Foreign Affairs in 1837 and had been in the original Herrera Cabinet of December, 1845.
8 General Manuel Gómez Pedraza was the leader of the moderate liberals. He had been President-elect in 1828 but owing to the fortunes of Mexican politics was unable to assume office until 1832. Until his death, in 1851, he played an important part in Mexican politics.
9 Valencia seems in general to have been an opportunist whose chief aim was to advance his own military power even at the expense of the nation's welfare.

are not going to weaken, because these outcries form their stock-in-trade. By this single act of his, he has succeeded in weakening his influence in the Government and has therefore deprived himself of any chance to speak in his own defense. He should have flung himself body and soul into the contest, since this would have been his only means of salvation. I do not have much confidence in his ability, but I think that he is much superior to the rest of those in the Government.

General Bustamante,[10] who has been accustomed to living in the President's palace, could not overcome his habits, which led him to be a daily caller on the President. This obliged him to espouse the President's cause and become one of his supporters. It is said today that he has grown very cool in his friendship with the President, and it is understood that he is on his way to Querétaro[11] to see a sister of his. General Bravo,[12] too, has left for Cuernavaca.[13]

I was assured this evening by a friend that a special messenger had arrived from San Luis at a business firm with news about Paredes's rebellion. He affirms this as an undeniable fact.

Today this bit of news, which has been going the rounds for the last several days, has assumed all the characteristics of the truth. It is said that the Government will proclaim the re-establishment of the Constitution of 1824[14] as soon as it receives word of Paredes's uprising, and that this was agreed upon with Farías,[15] the spokesman for the federalist faction. Con-

10 General Anastasio Bustamante had been active in Mexican politics for some time and had been President in 1830 and in 1837. He was associated with the conservatives.

11 City in the state of Querétaro. It is approximately 150 miles northwest of Mexico City.

12 General Nicolás Bravo was a conservative in politics from the time of Mexican independence until his death in 1854. Besides his military activities he had been Vice-president in 1824 and acting President in 1842 and in July and August, 1846.

13 City in the state of Morelos approximately forty-five miles south of Mexico City.

14 The Constitution of 1824 was federalistic. The constitution under which the Government was then functioning had been promulgated in 1843 and was known as the *Bases Orgánicas de la República Mexicana*. It was centralistic and gave broad powers to the executive. Although not a hard and fast rule of Mexican politics, generally those men holding liberal views were more likely to favor a federalistic form of Government which gave the states more power, while those with conservative opinions were in favor of a centralized Government. There were, in addition, two main factions within the liberal element: the group favoring radical reforms was known as the *puros* and the group which advocated gradual changes was known as the *moderados*.

15 Valentín Gómez Farías was one of the outstanding liberals of nineteenth century Mexico. His attempted clerical and educational reforms in 1833-34 led to his exile. He was back in Mexico in the late 1830s, then left again only to return in the 1840s. As the leader of the radical liberal party he did his best to try to overthrow Herrera, even going to the extent of writing to Paredes and suggesting that they correspond. Once Paredes was successful, however, Farías turned against him, believing his revolt only a military one. His dislike of the Herrera Government was based on his belief that Herrera would compromise Mexico on the

sidering the Cabinet's petty politics, I do not believe it to be impossible. It will mean the downfall of the Cabinet. It is a fact that a few days ago Farías had an interview with the Minister of War, and the latter was satisfied.

Saturday, the 20th

At dawn today the Government received a special communication sent by the Governor of Querétaro informing it of the insurrection led by Paredes. Pedraza told me that last night he sent a letter he had received from San Luis to the President which contained the same information. The President replied that he did not believe it. The Minister of War, who shared the same incredulity, said that it was *some kind of business scheme*. This must appear to be incredible!

The ministers came to the chambers to give an account of the happenings, and there was a great to-do. Navarro and Chico,[16] among others, got up on the speaker's rostrum and called Paredes a scoundrel, a traitor, and a drunken sot. In the galleries there were shouts of "Hurrah!" and "Down with Paredes!" and a motion was passed empowering the Government to declare the city in a state of siege. The ministers urged the Chamber to issue a manifesto, as a result of which Rosas, Ximénez, and Navarro were nominated to draw it up. The congressmen from San Luis protested in the name of their department against their Government's adhesion to Paredes, alleging duress.

Shortly after two o'clock in the afternoon the ministers appeared in the Senate Chamber. The galleries were crowded, and some of the deputies were in the crowd. The Minister of War [Don Pedro M. Anaya] read the plan,[17] commenting on the probable results, and in the name of the Government declared that it was resolved to pursue a constitutional course *and to bury itself beneath the ruins of the constitution*. He repeated this statement in other words with a sort of affectation which seemed to me destined to destroy the validity of his original one. I had thought that one very worth while because we could have escaped the dilemma by proclaiming a federation. If the Government had stated this very thing at the proper time and in clear language, it might have obtained valuable aid; but its wavering, obscure tactics have brought down upon its head innumerable difficulties. It has alienated many who were its friends. It has made its enemies hard to identify. It has intimidated those who might have been able to help it, and, of course, it has put to flight those who do not like to take risks. To climax its blunders, it has insulted and alienated a thousand men whom Reyes Veramendi had gathered about him. The Government is forced to rely on

Texan question and also that Herrera would not bring about a federalistic constitution. An invaluable aid in studying the Mexico of this period is C. A. Hutchinson *Valentín Gómez Farías, A Biographical Study* (Unpublished Ph.D. Thesis, University of Texas, Austin, Texas, 1948).

16 Both Suárez Navarro and Chico Sein were prominent congressmen.
17 Issued by Paredes at the time of his revolt.

troops of the garrison, which, it is said, it cannot trust. This suspicious fear has come too late, and I have grave misgivings that it will finally mean the Government's downfall. The imprudent ovation accorded the Fourth Infantry was the germ of discontent that will bear fruit in the splitting up of the garrison.

Pedraza is indeed a mere child when it comes to the most significant feature of politics: that of managing and knowing men. While the Minister of War was reading his account, Don Ramón Malo whispered in my ear, *"Don't tear into the Government!"*[18] He was recalling the severe criticism I had made of the ministers because of their indolence and incompetence two months before. I had predicted the very thing that has happened to them, and I had gone so far as to tell them that they would awake from their stupor only when the enemy was pounding upon the very doors of the Cathedral. The Government could not appreciate what I said, and it and its hangers-on treated me with distrust and coldness, if they did not actually treat me as an enemy. Well, Pedraza approached me yesterday to induce me to take the floor in defense of the Government and to express my anger against Paredes! I do not approve of his insurrection because I do not believe him to be the man of the hour, nor do I see any guarantee in his promises. But, on the other hand, I could not raise my voice in defense of a Government that has hatched and fostered this revolution by its scandalous apathy. Paredes is right in everything he says against Congress and the Government, because they both have behaved in the very same manner. They have rendered worthless the brilliant accomplishments of a glorious revolution[19] and have provided the staunchest argument against the representative system. The men who have taken advantage of the sixth of December constitute the symbol of ineptitude in politics.

Pedraza got up on the speaker's rostrum and made an imprudent harangue or, rather, delivered a most cruel philippic against Paredes. This will cost him dearly if we suffer defeat. He said there was no infamy in surrendering to a great genius like Napoleon, Caesar, Ghengis Khan, etc., but that it would be a mark of indelible insult for Mexico to find herself defeated by a rascal like Paredes. *"He is more of a rascal than I am,"*[20] he added; and after this silly comparison he went on to make a word-for-word commentary on Paredes's proclamation, thereby causing the galleries to burst into laughter. The deputies, at least, had fulfilled their own destinies by making the people furious. The session terminated with a fine speech by the President of the Senate [Barruecos] in reply to the ministers. But he did not take up the suggestion the latter had made concerning the issuance of a manifesto by the Chamber.

18   *"No vaya U. a darle una sacudida al gobierno."*
19   The revolution which led to the overthrow of Santa Anna on December 6, 1844.
20   *"es mas miserable que yo."*

In this great emergency the Government has shown its usual incapacity. The Minister of Foreign Affairs, Peña y Peña,[21] on behalf of the President urged the senators not to leave Mexico City during the conflict because His Excellency felt obliged to rely frequently upon their wise counsel, etc. This was a thoroughly stupid suggestion, since, on the face of it, it was offensive to the senators, and, to judge from its results, it was impertinent in the bargain. The Government, after securing sufficient power to avert the tempest, should urge them to get as far away as possible.

The second preliminary session could not be held.

They say that General Bravo has raised the standard of revolt. It may not be at all impossible, if it is true, that General Alvarado and his troops have been summoned.

Paredes's plan has been published in today's papers. I have observed that it does not satisfy anyone, and rightly so. In everything pertaining to politics he is extremely vague, being explicit only in his inclination to establish a military government. In his speech, Pedraza said that he had reliable facts warranting him in denouncing the plan as one intended to set up a foreign monarchy. Some people of good judgment believe the same thing. I cannot understand it, because the plan either conceals a profound mystery, which has not yet been revealed, or it is the attempt of a madman. At any rate, I can foresee that we shall not be able to escape a crisis; should this prove to be true, the resulting government would fall of its own weight, perhaps giving an opportunity for the return of General Santa Anna.

It is asserted that an English business firm has offered money to Paredes. I do not doubt it. We are in a situation in which we must definitely settle the question of Texas, California, and New Mexico [sic]. The American Minister, Slidell, is here and he can see with his own eyes that Mexico cannot possibly defend its territory.

Under these circumstances, Paredes has acted improperly in raising the standard of rebellion. On the speaker's rostrum, Pedraza charged that it was because he was afraid of going to Texas. I think that he was afraid because a policy of federation had been proclaimed in the capital and also because the presidential election had made him resentful and jealous.[22] This being the case, the Government is entirely to blame. It could not and would not be frank, as I have said before; and, in addition, it had developed a selfish fondness for its privileged position. I have been saying all along, however, that this uprising was planned for the sole purpose of calling a new election. I am convinced that I was not mistaken. Valencia, Almonte,[23] and

21 Manuel de la Peña y Peña was associated with the more conservative faction of the moderate liberals. He had been active in Mexican politics since independence and had, in 1837, held the post of Minister of Justice and Ecclesiastical Affairs under the Presidency of Bustamante.

22 An election had been held on August 1, 1845, at which time Herrera was chosen President. Previously he had held the office as an appointee of the Congress.

23 Juan N. Almonte served as an aide-de-camp to Santa Anna in the Texan War. He became increasingly prominent in Mexican affairs, and when Santa Anna returned to Mexico from his exile in Cuba in September, 1846, Almonte was a

even Paredes himself had agreed to maintain the *status quo* if General Bravo were elected President. It was planned thus not because of Bravo's ability but because he could be used as a sort of buffer to keep their jealousies quiet. Events have taken a new turn, and those jealousies will burst forth in due season. Almonte and Valencia have had a secret reconciliation that will add strength to their opponent's rebellion.

We have been asked to attend an extraordinary session at nine o'clock in the morning.

The authorities in Guanajuato and Querétaro have indicated that they do not favor the plan. The Government of Guanajuato says that its generalissimo (Don Teófilo Romero) is also against it. But I fear that there is a mystery behind all this. The Government and the Legislature of Querétaro have expressed opposition. The Supreme Court has followed suit.

Sunday, the 21st

The session called for nine o'clock did not begin until half-past eleven. I can sense a decided lack of enthusiasm. It is a pity that the summons was provoked by a truly ridiculous and impolitic event. Deputy Alas, who last year sided with Llaca in making accusations against General Santa Anna, today confused the time and the occasion by expressing the belief that a similar *coup d'état* could be carried out by accusing Paredes. He and my compatriot,[24] Hernández, made accusations against the Senate, and the President was indiscreet enough to convene the members to consider the charges. The senators took this accusation in a bad spirit because of its ridiculous tone. Political events are not just theatrical productions staged for entertainment. The accusation was ordered sent to the meeting of the members of the jury.[25] They will take care not to expedite matters. This event, of no consequence in itself, may very well change in aspect and end by getting us all involved.

The Chamber of Deputies was called into session to deliberate on the matter, and the Senate likewise was held in session to listen to speeches.

A friend of mine who always furnished me with reliable information said that he had planned to leave the city, but that someone persuaded him not to and assured him that there will be no disturbance because the garrison will join the revolutionary movement as soon as Paredes approaches the city. I am very much afraid that this is what will happen, to judge from the city's apathy and the confusion among those in the Government.

The Senate, summoned to hear the speeches, convened about nine o'clock. The Government was accorded constitutional powers to make arrests without legal formalities.

member of his Cabinet. He later was one of the leaders in obtaining French intervention in Mexico.

24 *"paisano,"* i.e., from the state of Durango.

25 When such an accusation was made, a committee of the Legislature would make a report on the charges. Following this, the Legislature would constitute itself into a jury to hear and decide on the accusation.

Monday, the 22nd

The preliminary session of the new Senate was convened very late because of the failure of the members to arrive on time. The old members were not more punctual.

The Senate approved the bill passed by the Chamber of Deputies condemning the authors and supporters of the insurrection and punishing them with the loss of their jobs.

The pamphlets and papers sent from San Luis were received. Among them was a stupid, foolish letter written by the President to Paredes in which it appears obvious that the Government, thanks to the dilatory tactics adopted to isolate Paredes, was not pushing the Texas conflict. The Government committed an impolitic act in opening a letter that had arrived for General Reyes[26] and in handing it to him without sealing it again.

I do not put much trust in the morale of the garrison.

A night session was called to discuss the revenue proposal. Cowed by the brokers,[27] the Chamber of Deputies has taken advantage of the needs of the country to surrender to them the wealth of the Californias[28] and all that they have stolen. The Senate committee, which had been assigned the task of delivering the speeches, met three hours later and argued the matter until after ten o'clock without getting anywhere. The Minister of Finance came in and pointed out the helplessness to which the Government has been reduced. It has no money or credit and not even energy enough to get them. It does not dare to take the slightest step unless a law has been previously enacted giving it authority to do so. Furthermore, it is the servant of the brokers in the Chamber of Deputies. There are endless arguments, and nobody thinks of anything else.

General Bustamante has returned and is evidently on the side of the Government.

There is not a trace left of that public spirit of a year ago. The press is almost silent.

Tuesday, the 23rd

A meeting of the committee was scheduled for ten o'clock, and it finally met around twelve. For three hours we argued with the Chamber of Deputies to save the riches of the Californias but we made no headway. I proposed that we exclude them from the law, but the suggestion was voted down. Their plan as approved is an insane piece of business which they will doubtless carry out, thereby forcing the Senate to the severe alternative of either sanctioning it or permitting the revolution to triumph.

The preparatory commission of the Chamber of Deputies is trying to destroy that body. It is bent upon annulling the Guadalajara elections

26 General Isidro Reyes had been Minister of War in 1844.
27 "*agiotistas.*"
28 As far as the editor could discover, this reference is to the pledging of Mexican Government holdings in California in order to obtain a loan from the brokers.

when it scarely has a quorum, and, at the same time, some of the members want to approve the election of Otero[29] in the face of his own statement that he is not of legal age. He himself has stirred up all these arguments, thus demonstrating that he is not a very sensitive individual.

The members of the Committee on Ways and Means attended the evening speeches, and there were tiresome discussions in trying to settle the matter so that the stupid action of the Chamber of Deputies could be ignored. Realizing that this was impossible and that the circumstances were urgent, they concluded the meeting by proposing that the Government be given ample powers to secure everything it might require, and that no one was to be liable to censure. Some members opposed this on the grounds that a pretense was being sought to save the Government by miracles without causing anyone any inconvenience. Trigueros,[30] Pardio, Mora, and Canalizo[31] have consistently absented themselves from these night sessions. Couto[32] got out of the meeting on the excuse that he was indisposed. I am afraid that in a critical situation there will not be a quorum. I find some of the senators quite timid and uninterested.

During this session the aforementioned law was passed, as were also the following measures: the date was set for filling vacancies left by senators not attending preliminary conferences, and the Government was authorized to declare the city in a state of siege. A chairman was appointed to head the committee charged with acquainting the other Chamber with the first of these proposals. Malo made a motion that the Senate issue a manifesto and that I be appointed chairman to draw it up. This was unthinkable. For a week I have been working day and night on administrative affairs, and they want to put on my shoulders all the new tasks that come along. I opposed this suggestion quite vehemently, appealing to the Chamber's sense of fair play, so Cuevas, Rodríguez Puebla, and Malo were appointed in my place.

Today the uproar caused by Deputy Navarro's incautious conduct finally reached a climax. In his tirade at the session on the twentieth, he included the army, calling it corrupt, etc., etc., and added that it must be destroyed. Reports of this incident reached even the common soldiers. They are talking about going over to Paredes *who,* as they declare, *is coming to defend them.* Yesterday Navarro printed an apology in the *Tribuna.*[33] This

29 Mariano Otero was associated with the moderate liberal group. Ramírez's opinion of him does not improve.

30 Ignacio Trigueros apparently was close to Gómez Farías in this period.

31 General Valentín Canalizo generally worked in close cooperation with Santa Anna. Hutchinson states that Herrera had imprisoned Canalizo in August. Hutchinson, *Gómez Farías,* 572. His political career had included the office of acting President from September, 1843, to September, 1844.

32 Bernardo Couto, a conservative moderate, had been in the cabinet of Herrera. Couto, an unusually interesting individual, was one of the first to occupy himself with the history of painting in Mexico.

33 Although the editor was unable to verify it, the *Tribuna* must have been a newspaper in Mexico City.

will not be as effective as the tirade was, nor will it be as quickly spread abroad. There is not a single person who speaks favorably of the Government, and this includes even the friends of the Government and its own agents, like Pedraza, Monjardín, and others. The more moderate men, like Cuevas and Couto, are not saying anything. If the Government is saved, it will be a miracle and will be the sole result of the instinct for republicanism. If Paredes had confined his efforts merely to a demand for a house-cleaning, the result would be a foregone conclusion.

Up to the present hour, we have been getting news about the resistance offered by the legislatures of Guanajuato, Querétaro, and Puebla.

The Government has begun to exercise its discretionary powers. Tonight it arrested Lombardo, Villamil, Sierra y Roso, Franco and his son, and General Gutiérrez.[34]

Valencia has returned from his country residence and has had a conference with the President. No one knows the present mood of the Government or how it will act. It is maintaining an obstinate silence. This is a bad sign.

Wednesday, the 24th

I took to the Chamber of Deputies the report agreed upon concerning ways and means. Article Two was rejected. This article had been slyly inserted and dealt with the case of the brokers who had seized the finances of the Californias. The Chamber voted to accept the report as originally agreed upon.

The more I think about this peculiar insurrection the more I have come to believe that through some mistake we are going to be lost. It seems to me that Paredes started his revolt because he feared that Congress would proclaim the federation. Even those of us who are on the scene come to the same conclusion. Congress has decreed otherwise; now what turn will the insurrection take?

Santa Anna's followers are going to attain their goal by investing Paredes with the political power which they had formerly given the Government. It has all been the fault of the Government, because a simple statement in the *Diario* would have cleared up these misunderstandings. What this apparently insignificant newspaper has already done, and can still do! If Paredes wins I am sure that his defeat will be a certainty, since the return of the exiles is inevitable.

Today I received a copy of the proceedings involving Barranda,[35] who was indicted by the decree dissolving Congress. How will this case be settled if Paredes wins? I recall the deep truth contained in an epigram which Michelena quoted one day when he saw the justices of the Supreme Court enter the hall where we were meeting: "These gentlemen have been given power to pass judgment on defeated revolutionaries."

---

34 General José Ignacio Gutiérrez was later to serve as Minister of War in March, 1847.
35 Ramírez later goes into more detail on Manuel Barranda's position.

This is a terrible observation to make, and it obliges me to conclude that there must be some great error in the conventional way of judging political causes.

Thursday, the 25th

Don Pedro Lemus and Eligio Romero have been arrested, and a search is on for Don Lorenzo Carrera. It is said that Almonte has gone into hiding. Carrera was the instigator of last year's insurrection. Profiting by his friendship with S.A.[36] he induced the latter to give Paredes the command in Sonora[37] in order to afford him the opportunity and means to start a revolution. I sympathized with this movement in all good faith; but I shall never approve such treacherous and infamous methods as the one I have just described.

The mail has arrived. Events are moving very slowly. It was revealed that Paredes was probably still in San Luis on the twenty-first and had sent General Gaiferos against Guanajuato.

The city has been declared in a state of siege. We were summoned to an extraordinary night session. It was raining hard, and a cold wind was blowing. Nevertheless I attended, although I was certain that there would be no session. As a matter of fact, only fourteen of us met.

The Chamber of Deputies has insisted on carrying out its illegal and shameful plan to provide revenues for the Government. Escandón, the broker-deputy, has succeeded in controlling the Chamber, forcing the Senate to the severe alternative of either sanctioning his thefts or leaving the Government without resources, a ready prey to the revolution. The Minister of Finance [Castillo] appeared at the committee meeting to defend the Chamber of Deputies and to give authentic testimony of his administrative incapacity. He rejected the authorization agreed upon by the Senate, stating *that it was so vague and so general that the Government would find itself embarrassed in its efforts to carry it out, since by virtue of this authorization it could not only dispose of these funds, but even of private property in the event that it might wish to take advantage of its powers, and would thereby alarm the citizens,* etc. He said this at the very time that the Government was bewailing its total lack of resources and the straitened circumstances in which the insurrection was placing it. What other man in his position could have said such things!

But it is perfectly obvious that he was the man who asked that the restrictions be increased after he had been given the power to float a loan of fifteen millions, and all the while fought any increase in funds proposed by the committee. He is also a member of that same group which after December 6 got the Congress to pass the restrictions on the veto.

In the Chamber of Deputies and in the Senate these men have reached

36 Text, in a footnote, states: Santa Anna. Use of the initials continues throughout the book.
37 State in northern Mexico.

an impasse which they themselves created and today they discover that they are being hanged in their own noose. Both Chambers admit as a truth of political faith that the power of Congress to revise the contracts made by General S. A. emanates directly from the Plan of Tacubaya;[38] that the legislative branch of the Government does not have this inherent power; that the plan, outranking all the laws and the powers of the Government, grants Congress this year as the limit for its exercise of the power of revision. The time having elapsed, the contracts will be for that very reason ratified, and then there will be no longer any power to change them. The deputies have taken advantage of this provision, which is absurd, antisocial and prejudicial to the very dignity of the legislative power itself, to foist this law upon the Senate and thus assure the triumph of the brokers. Under the pretext of the emergency confronting the Government and the impossibility of making a revision of the law within the six days still remaining, they are forcing the Senate to approve the bill passed by the Chamber of Deputies; and the senators are falling into the trap.

Couto and Pedraza attempted to reach an agreement with the committee from the Chamber of Deputies and brought back a silly article in which a few words are changed but which leaves the situation the same. In this bill the funds of the Californias and the hospitals remain alienated and incorporated in the public treasury, contrary to what was expressly stated in a previous agreement, which the deputies arbitrarily ordered filed away. The alternative facing us is horrible: we shall either have to satisfy the voracity of the brokers, or put the Government under the knife of the revolution. I have resisted to the last and have confined myself to voting against the proposal, explaining that I did so because I considered the proposal unconstitutional. It will not be long ere they raise an outcry against me in the other Chamber.

Our authorization, which the Minister had rejected as vague, was as follows: *The Government is authorized for the term of one month to provide itself with the necessary revenues in order to preserve and defend the constitutional system of the Republic.* The Minister agreed with another suggestion that would exclude the funds set aside for the departments and for payment on the debt. Both points are absurd. The first because the revolution is not aimed at the destruction of the central Government, which, in any event, it is bound to destroy. It is, however, aimed at destroying the governments of the departments, and, as a result, it is absurd to withhold state revenues from the amount designated for general expenditures. The second point is equally foolish because Minister Rosa[39] had pledged future revenues very heavily, and there are no free funds left. If in cases like the

38   The Plan of Tacubaya was promulgated on September 28, 1841. It brought about the overthrow of President Bustamante and allowed Santa Anna to take power.
39   Luis de la Rosa had been Minister of Finance in the provisional government from the end of March to August, 1845.

present one payment is not suspended, I do not know when such payment can ever be made. Everything tends to prove a sad and shameful state of affairs: that we are trained neither in theory nor in practice, nor do we have the virtues or the personal character demanded by a well-regulated system of representative government. Weak men, who are impressed more by individuals than by events; indolent men, who do not care to trouble themselves about thinking or working, and who vote without a conscience; these ought only to obey because they are unable to command. When a member of the established Government can express these melancholy opinions he can excuse Santa Anna and Paredes for their hatred of congresses.

In yesterday's *Siglo* the Government was frank enough to tell the people that the rebels had changed their plan. This is unbearable. The most significant feature of that plan was that it would have helped the Government by the very fear it inspired. But today the Government itself is calming the people's fears by offering hope. Great heavens, what stupidity!

Minister Montes de Oca called on a friend of his who is an *out-and-out supporter of Santa Anna* and asked this friend to keep some trinkets in his house, saying that he did not have any confidence in the Government's ability to see this thing through. Montes de Oca doubts the loyalty of the garrison and says that the ministers are busy discussing the best way to get out. This was said by a minister! And to a political opponent! He also said that the Cabinet was deliberating whether or not to arm the people, but that the members were afraid of them.

From the various bits of news I have received it seems that the morale of the troops is bad. This applies even to the famous Fourth Battalion itself. In a cafe I overheard some officers say that *although the Government had the Fourth Battalion on its side, it was a Figure Four Trap that Paredes had set.*[40] While these things have been going on a notice has appeared to the effect that Paredes's troops have occupied Guanajuato. *Don Luis Cuevas* was one of those who gave out the information.

The memorandum dealing with the manifesto to be issued by the Senate was presented. This is a bit of the purest nonsense, filled with invective and with very little trace of sound reasoning. How many stupid things have been done with this purpose in mind! It all began by reading the memorandum in a public session, thereby rendering impossible any effort to amend it. Señor Navarrete, who is fast going into his second childhood, immediately moved that the memorandum be signed by all the senators. As was to be expected, the motion carried. This bit of business has produced a terrible misunderstanding and hostility, because there are many senators who are

40   The text reads: "aunque el Gob⁰. tenía al n⁰. 4, era un cuatro que Paredes había al Gobierno." Here the term "era un cuatro" indicates a pun on the number four, referring in the first instance to the Fourth Battalion, and in the second case, to the type of trap known as the Figure Four Trap, in which the working parts to be sprung are arranged in that figure. The meaning, of course, is that Paredes will march to the capital and cause the Fourth Battalion to desert to him.

partisans of Santa Anna, and in the memorandum he is criticized severely. On the other hand there is much praise of the Government, and there are many who think this praise unjustified. Poor Trigueros found himself in a most desperate predicament, and some of the members advised him not to sign. Several others signed under protest, which greatly decreases the strength of the motion. All this was the work of Navarrete, who is the type of man to do such things. He also proposed that the minutes of the discussion [about the organization of the departments] be printed. This was a very foolish thing to do, because those opposed to the motion had previously refused to discuss the matter, presuming that there would be no debate. But he is just a seventy-year-old child.

Some time ago a friend of mine told me that a committee meeting had been held in the President's Palace. Among those present was Monjardín. The purpose of the meeting was to agree upon the proclamation of the Constitution of 1824 as soon as the opportunity presented itself. I did not believe this at the time, but Monjardín himself confirmed it for me today. He assured me that the Chamber of Deputies (or, rather, the half which remains) had agreed on the matter, and the proclamation would be issued the first of next month. On this basis we can explain easily Paredes's plan, which wishes to retain neither the present system nor the one soon to be promulgated.

Saturday, the 27th

They say that there has been an uprising in Veracruz and that the rebels have sent the steamer *Moctezuma* to Havana to bring back General S. A. The whole situation looks quite natural and logical to me. I was also informed last night that the United States had made proposals to S. A. with a view toward reinstating him, provided that he would recognize the independence of Texas, and that he refused, saying that he would return only if he were recalled by the spontaneous vote of the people.

The members of the Cabinet appeared before the Chamber to give an account of the events in Veracruz. The uprising started at the fort[41] and then, *like lightning,* so the report goes, involved the troops of the garrison in the city. General Landero[42] put himself at the head of the rebels, and the insurrection left General Noriega without means of defense. He has remained loyal and has started out with a small detachment of light infantry to join Inclán. Captain Guzmán, one of the instigators of the revolt, was killed in the skirmishing. The revolt began on the twenty-third at noon when the troops were on their way here. There was also an uprising in Jalapa,[43] and they say the same thing has occurred in Perote.[44] The Minister

41 San Juan de Ulúa.
42 General José Juan Landero was later to be the Mexican General in command of Veracruz when the city surrendered to the Americans in 1847.
43 A city in the state of Veracruz approximately seventy-five miles inland and up high enough to be out of the fever zone.
44 A town a short distance west of Jalapa and, like Jalapa, on the road to Puebla and Mexico City from the coast.

of War says that he still has loyal troops here and in Puebla and declares that the city will be defended to the last. I distrust all the troops. Knowing the situation as I do, I am convinced that the Government will fall as soon as Paredes approaches the city.

At one o'clock this morning, and quite accidentally, another attempt at insurrection was put down. If it had succeeded it might have put an end to the uncertainty. General Ampudia, in agreement with Oronoz, the colonel from Celaya, marched the battalion out of its barracks, stating that orders had been received from General Bustamante to go to the *Ciudadela*.[45] Actually they were going there for the purpose of taking it by surprise. The troops themselves knew nothing about this plan, and it seems that many of the officers likewise were not in on the secret. They unexpectedly came upon the officer of the day, Don N. Barrios, who ordered them to halt. He was not satisfied with the alleged order said to have been received from the General-in-Chief and commanded the battalion to return to the barracks, adding that he would not permit the order to be carried out because it had been issued without his knowledge. Ampudia and Oronoz were bewildered, and, instead of seizing Barrios, started to run away. The plot was thereby revealed and suppressed. No trace has been found of the ringleaders; but the fact that they are still in Mexico City and that they made this attempt are indicative of evil events to come.

The President of the Senate has arranged for the approval of the budget and senators' pay, giving as his reason the fact that today's session might perhaps be the last.

The Government leaders sent the following requests for the election of senators:

Chamber of Deputies: General Don Pedro de Anaya, the lawyer Cordero, the lawyer Fernández de Castro.

Government: General Don Isidro Reyes, Deputy Don Luis Solana, the lawyer Don Miguel Atristaín.

Supreme Court: General Don Martín Carrera, the lawyer Don Mariano Domínguez, the lawyer Don N. Fernández de Castro.

The Senate appointed the first three nominees, taking into consideration the fact that they are still senators, that they have conducted themselves in an exemplary fashion, and that under the circumstances it would be an affront to the nominees and an act full of danger to the public interest to ignore them. There is no doubt whatsoever that circumstances always decide the course of action. In a preliminary session we elected some men senators although obviously they were not qualified, either legally or otherwise. Why? Because there was an insufficient number for the installation of the Chamber. Not one of the newly appointed senators has appeared because of the

---

45 The Ciudadela was a fort and an arsenal in Mexico City. It was generally the headquarters of the commandant of Mexico City and thus it had been the scene of many uprisings.

threat of revolution. This single factor is an incontestable argument against the Republic and the representative system of government.

An additional article to the constitution was approved today. With honest and intelligent administration it would be a means of saving the Government. It provides that if the Congress cannot open its sessions or cannot assemble at the time set by the constitution, another date is to be set by Congress itself. Should Congress be unable to do so the permanent committee of Congress will act. If there is no committee then the duty falls on the President.

Today I began to lay in a supply of provisions in case there should be a conflict in the city, although my personal opinion is that the disloyalty of the troops will make this precaution unnecessary. I do not believe that the soldiers will revolt to defend this or that system of government but because they are afraid of having to fight. Baseness and corruption have reached such a stage that any movement for revolt now is assured of success because of the simple fact that it is such a movement.

Several booths have been set up in various parts of the city to enlist volunteers.

The civil authorities in Veracruz have declared themselves opposed to the revolution.

As I was leaving the house this evening I heard newsboys shouting "Bulletin *from the Government* announcing the Veracruz uprising! Militia now called up!" Two powerful incentives calculated to win the rebel soldiers back to the Government side! The Government has encouraged the revolt down to the present moment by its use of the most inappropriate frankness.

I happened to fall in with a group of enthusiastic federalists, among whom were several deputies. They were roundly criticizing the Government for its inefficiency and were blaming it for having tricked them by throwing itself into the arms of the Scottish Rite Masons.[46] It would appear that the Government was to have proclaimed the federation on the 6th of December but was dissuaded from doing so by the Masons, who claimed that such a procedure was revolutionary in character and that it was a bad example to set at the very time legal means were being sought to maintain public order. Finally it was proposed that federation could be established later by the authority of the Congress itself so that everything would be strictly legal. The fact that the Masons *won't choose sides* is the basis for incriminating them. Such inaction makes the federalists assume that they wish to let the revolution drag on, thereby preventing the establishment of permanent order. These events are quite naturally connected with others to which I have already referred and which are convincing proof that a formal agreement was made to proclaim the federation. One of the men in the group asked me if I did not think that there was still time to do this in order to

46 *Escoceses.* They were more conservative than the York Rite Masons (*Yorkinos*).

save the situation. I replied that since matters had gone so far I was of the opinion such an act would only complicate things and result in useless sacrifice. The truth is that our social organization is not steady on its foundations.

This group of federalists also told me that owing to popular opinion the plan of the revolution had been changed in the manner mentioned above and that the new executive power was assigned to Valencia, Bravo, and Paredes. In the Cabinet the posts are to be filled by Almonte, Foreign Affairs; Tornel,[47] War; and Garay,[48] Treasury. I suppose Castillo will be appointed Minister of Justice and I am very much afraid that Lombardo will be elected in the place of the legal candidate.

A certain Casanova was one of the ringleaders of the uprising in Veracruz. Being a vehement Santa Anna partisan, he was a forgotten man after the revolution and was a sick one in the bargain. Pedraza vouched for him so that he would be permitted to go to Veracruz and later interceded so that the army reinstated him. If Pedraza escapes from his present predicament he ought to renounce politics forever, for his own good and that of the country. Our soldiers have lost all sense of honor, loyalty, and gratitude. What governs their behavior? Only selfishness.

Sunday, the 28th

The preliminary session of the Senate, called for eleven o'clock, convened at two, with General Bustamante present. It had been necessary to recall him from active duty with the troops. Molinos del Campo was absent because *he had gone to Mixcoac to spend a day in the country.* Almonte presided but he reminded us that he had been ill for the past several days. Riva Palacio[49] was absent and was also ill. The Archbishop remained in Tacubaya.[50] This prelate is doing a very foolish thing in not coming to the sessions, since public opinion has set him down as a champion of the revolution and monarchy.

The Senate chose Pimentel as its President and Don Rafael Espinosa and Pacheco as secretaries. Pedraza bossed this election, and I presume that there was some purpose behind the choice of Pimentel. Perhaps he was selected because he is shy, which will prevent him from settling disputes, and on the other hand he has shown that he can be calm and firm.

For the past three days the activities in the Ministry of Foreign Affairs have been paralyzed because of the illness of the Minister [Peña y Peña] and the Undersecretary [Ortiz Monasterio]. The Ministers of the Treasury and Justice could not be found today. Their presence was necessary to

47 General José María Tornel y Mendívil in general favored Santa Anna. Yet he was always careful enough to assure himself a high Government position, even if it meant turning against Santa Anna.

48 Antonio Garay was friendly with Gómez Farías.

49 Mariano Riva Palacio was an outstanding leader in nineteenth century Mexico and generally well respected by both the extreme right and extreme left. He was the father of the equally famous Vicente Riva Palacio. All references to "Riva Palacio" in this work are to Mariano.

50 Suburb of Mexico City.

enable the President to receive the committees from the two Chambers. These committees were to advise him that the Congress was installed. Only the Minister of War has shown up. I am amazed at how we can keep a semblance of public order.

The enlistments of volunteers for the defense of the city have been slow and scanty.

We have had news about the uprisings in Guadalajara, Aguascalientes and Zacatecas.[51] It will not be strange if the Government hurries to publish this news as it did that about the Veracruz disturbances. Only a miserable handful of troops revolted in the cities just named, the civil authorities offering no more than token resistance. The whole affair is quite clear, and no one can deceive himself. It is war between the soldiers and the civil authority.

We know that Paredes's advance units are due to arrive in Tula[52] today. General Bustamante has expressed his determination to resist, and several military men say that if the troops of the garrison remain loyal, Paredes will certainly be defeated. I have no confidence in the troops.

Monday, the 29th

A.[53] came to see me, and I thought his visit quite mysterious. The account he gave me of our situation is discouraging. He had come from the home of General Bustamante, and according to what the General told him it seems he has no other hope than to die in the coming conflict. "I am old," the General said. "I have no family nor any attachments and can wish for nothing better than to die with a bullet in me. At the last minute we have armed the populace, and this has excited and angered the troops. My greatest worry now is how to control the situation so that there will not be a clash. Since no judgment was used in arming the people I have very grave fears that they will indulge in all kinds of excesses, thus repeating the scenes of 1828. In that event I shall be occupied in controlling the mob and I shall even send troops against them if need be." The people share the same fears, which are cooling all enthusiasm for resistance and facilitating the triumph of Paredes. If the Government had ordered the militia to be armed immediately after the victory of December 6 the outcome might be different. But by following in the fooststeps of its predecessor and with less prestige and power over the army, the present Government made an effort to rely on the handful of troops still loyal to it and refused to put any confidence in the nation, to which it owed its amazing triumph.

Almonte talked to me about coming to some understanding on a method of action that would produce some semblance of order, excluding any consideration of the legality of such action, and several times gave me to understand that my influence might be decisive in the matter. I could not un-

51 Both Aguascalientes and Zacatecas are the capitals of states of the same name. Both states are located in north central Mexico.
52 Town in the state of Hidalgo just north of Mexico City.
53 Probably Almonte.

derstand what he was driving at, because although I urged him to explain the projected plan of action more clearly, he replied that it was too confused at the moment for him to discuss it. In order to see if I could draw him out a bit I suggested that I did not see how anything could be accomplished in the Senate as it is now constituted, and he then told me he was hoping for better results from the future Senate. I suppose that there is some scheme on foot for a new arrangement of things, and perhaps I have been tested to get my ideas about the election of a President who will lend the proper atmosphere to a new administration.

Today's session did not take up anything of importance.

It was suggested that we consider the Chamber of Deputies' resolution rejecting the treaties with Yucatán.[54] I was opposed to the resolution, arguing that it would alienate the good will of Yucatán and that, left in its present form, it would provide a great obstacle for anyone who might try to take it up later. The matter was allowed to remain unchanged.

The Mercantile Tribunal[55] announced that the necessary orders had been given to pay Couto his daily fee according to a Senate agreement. It is to be regretted that this body has soiled its hands at the last minute by such a foul injustice that contributes directly to the betrayal of the two consulting attorneys. [See the appendix for an account of this transaction.][56]

We are due to end our sessions tomorrow, and I am very much afraid that someone else will compel us to do so before twenty-four hours have passed. They say that Paredes's advance troops are three leagues away and that he is on his way to Tacubaya to put himself at the head of the rebellious garrison there. I think the plan is sure to succeed, although it may have very terrible results in the interior since the people are armed. Apparently the total enlistments have reached the 3,000 figure. Under other circumstances the present force would suffice to balk any attempt by Paredes; but today there are good reasons to fear that fighting will break out among the very defenders of the city themselves.

General Mora Villamil, who last year took up arms against S. A., is today leading the rebels in Veracruz. Anarchy is wide-spread among them, because half want S. A. to return and the others are against it. The same argument will soon appear in the rest of the army.

Some important people insist on believing that Paredes's activities are for the purpose of re-establishing a monarchy, since they say that for the past several years he has harbored Monarchist views. I cannot believe all

54 The peninsula had not agreed to a centralistic form of government, and like Texas, when its dislike of the central government became strong enough it rebelled. It had revolted in 1841 but had signed a treaty with Mexico in 1843 to come back into the union. The treaty had been on Yucatán's own terms, and the question here involved is one of accepting or rejecting this treaty.

55 Mercantile tribunals were established in 1841 in the capitals of the departments and in the ports open to foreign trade. Three men on each tribunal tried suits that concerned commercial transactions.

56 Not included in the García edition.

this because such a plan seems to me unworkable if it is carried out by a military coup. It could be successful only if brought about by intervention or conquest and it will come of its own accord if military anarchy follows the present unsettled situation.

Ricardo has come to tell me that public unrest is increasing, not on account of the enemy but rather on account of the defenders, since the commander of the troops quartered in San Pablo[57] stated that he cannot restrain them and that they are continually shouting, "Down with the Army!"

Ricardo has given me news that calls attention to the visit of A[lmonte]. I am beginning to suspect that the rebels are figuring on some sort of agreement with Bustamante to produce another Treaty of Estanzuela as a means of saving the city and getting some guarantees. When A. was talking to me about the new Senate I told him I lacked influence with the incoming members, and that at most I could rely on the old ones. He then complimented me and incidentally asked me if I were not a good friend of B.'s.[58] I told him I was, and the conversation stopped there. Of course, A. and B. have seen Bustamante frequently these last few days.

The mercantile group has put up posters calling upon all businessmen, farmers, and brokers to take up arms "because public order and the interests of the property-owning classes are in danger."

The *Siglo XIX* today publishes details of the stories given out by two deserters from the army in Texas concerning the situation there. This truly horrible carelessness has been frequently repeated in our country, for I have seen published even the information received from our spies living in enemy territory, together with their full names. The Minister of Finance has also published the notes he sent to the governors of the departments explaining to them the hopeless condition of our treasury in so far as aid for the operations against Texas are concerned. An example of this kind of stupidity can be found in Number 402 of the *Durango Register*.[59] In this country we have the strange knack of publishing things that it is not wise to make public, and of holding back information on matters that should be discussed. On one occasion the senators argued with Minister Peña about the desirability of publishing all the documents relative to the dispute with France over the *Baño de las delicias*[60] affair, then pending. The Minister wanted to give it to the press. Finally he published quite inopportunely the report in which the Council refused to accept the American Minister.

I feel sorry for Gómez Pedraza. His enemies make him out to be responsible for everything and manager of the Cabinet while he, as he himself declares, has clashed even with Señor Herrera, who has taken offense at

57 This apparently refers to a section of Mexico City.
58 Baranda?
59 *El Registro Oficial de Durango* was the official publication of the state of Durango.
60 The reference is to an incident which took place on the street named *Baño de las delicias*. Because of the incident the French Minister asked for his passport in May, 1845.

numerous bits of advice he has offered. These people also say that he engineered the selection of Montes de Oca. Today Pedraza in speaking of him told me that "all he was good for was a museum of natural history." I believe, nevertheless, that Pedraza is to blame for having withdrawn at the wrong time and in not knowing how to manitain the influence he once had. He should have broken openly with the Government when he saw that he was being ignored.

At this moment (seven o'clock in the evening) newsboys are in the streets, shouting about the Government's fifth bulletin which announces the arrival of Paredes in Cuautitlán![61] The Government has kept the presses rolling to tell the people about each one of its disasters. It could not have been done any better by agents of the rebellion whose newspapers the Government has ordered suppressed.

Tuesday, the 30th

It seems that my worst fears have been realized. Mounted sentries armed with carbines have been stationed at all points where the streets open upon the public squares, and while I was standing with a group of businessmen on the street below I was told that all the troops of the garrison, with the exception of those quartered in the President's Palace, had revolted at dawn this morning. Some in this same group declared that even General Bustamante had gone over to the rebels, although others contradicted them. Rumor has it that the troops defending the city are not at their posts.

The city presents an aspect of excitement and sadness. Carriages are leaving in all directions, and merchants are gathering in groups near their establishments, which they have closed. It seems to me impossible for this state of affairs to continue any longer than the year. I think that when Paredes gets near the city the uncertainty will end, or rather, his approach will consummate the revolution, rendering useless the resistance they say the Palace troops will put up. It has been ascertained that the General slept in Tanepantla[62] last night.

Valencia has raised the standard of revolt at the *Ciudadela*, and Tornel is with him. Gordoa refused to believe that the latter was one of the most active agents of the rebellion, basing his opinion on the fact the man never wanted to talk politics and on his lack of gravity, which was only assumed. At half-past one in the morning a cannon shot was heard from the *Ciudadela*, probably as a signal for the troops in the garrison.

At the present time (eight minutes to eleven) a page has come from the Senate to announce that a session has been called by the President of the Republic. But at the same time he brings the notice that no one will be permitted to enter the Palace, not even the deputies and senators, because *the troops of the loyal Fourth Battalion do not want Congress to meet*. The Battalion has also revolted, and the troops are remaining at their posts only

61 A town just northwest of Mexico City.
62 A town approximately fifteen miles northwest of Mexico City.

to keep order. I do not know what I ought to do in these circumstances, since in my judgment trying to summon Congress is the final piece of stupidity. What purpose can it serve? Perhaps to lend an appearance of legality to the revolt, which would be a stain that Congress would put on itself at the last moment. All in all, it would be better to let well enough alone.

They say that the troops defending Santo Domingo and San Francisco[63] will not put down their arms. All the others permitted themselves to be disarmed last night without a struggle.

Crowds are appearing again on the streets, and the city is going back to its customary ways. The people are surging into the public square to see what is going on, and perhaps to cheer their oppressors later on. At a quarter to eleven an alarm was sounded that sent the crowd scurrying in all directions, but it turned out to be false.

Quarter after eleven. Nothing can be done about the situation now. We must resolutely face the predicament into which the President of the Republic has plunged us with his foolish summons to convene. I cannot find even the slightest degree of propriety or advantage in his action. I am going to the Chamber.

Half-past one. I have come back from the Senate. Everything was done in the worst manner possible.

After I had reached the Palace door, of which only the shutter was open, the sentry put out his gun and barred my way. I insisted on going in, and he replied that he would not permit me to do so without authority from the officer of the guard, who, judging from the signals the sentry made, was standing among a group of officers some distance from the entrance. I was about to go over to them when I felt someone tap me on the shoulder. I turned around and saw an officer who asked me *if I were a deputy.* I told him in no uncertain terms that I was, and he quite courteously let me go in. The troops were under arms. Four cannon with fuses lighted barred the entrance way. Only three senators had appeared.

I learned that the militia defending the city had given up their arms and that Valencia had ordered them to remain in barracks to keep order.

At a quarter after twelve the President of the Chamber [Berruecos] had not yet arrived. General Reyes, who has taken a hand in the events, came in and told me that Valencia had sent a message to the President. In it he implied that the President should resign, accusing him of laxness in the prosecution of the war, etc., etc., and especially of frightening the city by arming the rabble. This last fact had made the rebels resolve to bring the matter to a decision in order to avoid a tragic situation and the shedding of blood. Valencia also sent the President a copy of the revised plan which can be reduced substantially to a few main points. A committee was to be organized consisting of six deputies, six senators, six members of the Advisory Council, two members of the Supreme Court, two from the Court *Marcial*[64] and two from the Assembly. The committee would have the following duties: first, to determine whether the executive power should be entrusted to one individual or to three; second, to appoint the triumvirs; and third, to set in motion the machinery for the election of a new Congress.

The Cabinet on this solemn occasion evinced the same incapacity with which it had conducted affairs from the beginning, since it replied that it was going to convene both Chambers immediately to place before them the matter of the President's resignation and ask for a discussion! This is indeed what one might call going to any lengths to make a mistake! Why was a session of the Chambers required? To sanction the revolt and stain Congress with an act of weakness? To make the Congress look foolish if the session were not held? Reyes told me that he had advised the ministers to submit calmly to force since they could not count on any means of defense and that in any event they should refrain from talking about resigning. No one paid any attention to him.

The troops surrounding us in the Palace had revolted but they said that they were determined to resist if any attempt were made to insult Señor Herrera. They were staying only to protect him.

Shortly after one o'clock an emissary arrived from the *Ciudadela*. The President of the Republic sent out an urgent order to find the Senate emissary but the latter had not yet arrived. Fortunately Reyes was present. He had served in that capacity the month before, which relieved me of having to discharge the duty, since I had served the month before that.

Reyes returned shortly and in a secret meeting with the others who were present told us on behalf of the President what has already been explained with regard to the plan. He added that the last envoy from the *Ciudadela* had brought the news that the command of the plaza had been turned over to General Salas,[65] who had relieved Peña y Barragán, and *that it was hoped that the President would take the whole thing in the proper spirit, since it was, after all, an act tempered with moderation*, etc. That is a delicate bit of consideration for you! The President was also informed that a Cabinet had been named consisting of the following men: War, Tornel; Foreign Affairs, Almonte; Finance, Garay; Justice, Bonilla.[66] The President had also been told that further information on other matters and on the final outcome would be sent that afternoon, after the anticipated arrival of Paredes! A fine state of affairs, indeed! A son without a father, or what is the same thing, a Cabinet sired without a President and govern-

64 The reference is probably to the *Suprema Corte Marcial* which was established in the 1830s, abolished in 1842 and reinstituted in 1845. It was composed of the regular members of the Supreme Court and several generals.

65 José Mariano Salas, supposedly faithful to Paredes, was later to work for the return of Santa Anna. After the overthrow of Paredes in August, 1846, Salas served as President for a brief period.

66 Probably Manuel Diaz de Bonilla who was a Santa Anna supporter.

ing before it has been given life! Reyes concluded by telling us that the President felt there was no hope of attaining a quorum in both Chambers since some members had been prevented from entering the Palace that morning. He therefore sent word to us that the session was closed. I asked Reyes to tell the President that no matter what happened not to consider again calling another session, because it would do nothing except help destroy the respectability of Congress.

Reyes, speaking *like a childish old man*, said that it was certain that the six deputies who were to be on the committee were already at the *Ciudadela*. Someone else added that the six senators were there, too. I doubt it.

I asked Reyes if General Bustamante had come out in support of the plan, and he replied *that the General had shown a decided coolness toward it*. I suppose that if he were undecided, it was the fact that the people had been armed which made him so.

The following persons attended this meeting at the Palace: Aguilera, Becerra, Carrera, Delmote,[67] García, Gómez de la Cortina, Malo, Madrid (the Bishop), Morales (Don Ramón), Monjardín, Navarrete, Pizarro, Quintana Roo, Ramírez, Robles, Rodríguez Puebla, Ruiz, Reyes, Segura, Urquiaga. Those who usually attended *but were not at this meeting* were: Aguirre, Berruecos (President), Canalizo, Couto, Cuevas, Espinosa de los Monteros, Gómez Anaya, Gómez Pedraza, Goribar, Guimbarda, Icaza, Irigoyen, Liceaga, Ormeacha, Pardio, Pérez Gálvez, Pimentel, Rosas (Secretary), Trigueros. It is very likely that Gómez Anaya and Liceaga were unable to attend because of illness. Gómez Pedraza had good reason not to come.

There was not a quorum in the Chamber of Deputies either, and the senior of our two deputies from Durango was absent.

In formulating the above lists I have taken into consideration the fact that six senators may have been at the *Ciudadela*. I shall refrain, however, from making any definite statement to that effect.

In the Senate they tell the following incident. A detachment of troops at Chapúltepec[68] revolted and loudly cheered Paredes, attempting at the same time to reach the summit of the hill on which the Military School stands. When the young cadets saw this they rushed to the redoubt and, facing the rebels, hauled up a cannon, giving cheers for the Congress. The regulars had to retreat and asked only that they be allowed to go without being attacked.

A quarter after three. The city has completely gone back to its customary life. There is no indication that an event fraught with such important consequences has transpired. *"Miseri homines ad servitutem parati!"*[69] as Tacitus would say. But as is now obvious, the people had neither leaders nor ideals to induce them to make the great sacrifice which was necessary.

67 Del Monte?
68 Chapúltepec Palace in Mexico City.
69 Wretched men, prepare to submit to slavery.

I am going out in the street to add to the number of imbeciles.

Shortly before four o'clock General Valencia entered the Palace with a large staff and then left for his home accompanied by an immense number of people. At the same time people who had gone up to the towers of the Cathedral and all the other churches started to ring the bells furiously by way of celebrating. Now try to believe in the sovereignty of the people! Strain your mental powers to the bursting point to find anything that can justify their actions! These citizens of ours are nothing but a flock of sheep that need the lash. They are good for nothing except to maintain a few ambitious and ignorant demagogues in power.

I met Senator Morales and settled a little matter that I had overlooked this morning. While the Senate was in session, he had come over to me to say that it would be advisable to put the rebellion on firm legal ground by proceeding to the election of the six senators to the committee, even if there were not a quorum. I did not agree with him because I was for exactly the contrary course of action. Now he has told me that he was working with Valencia, and that some man whom I did not know and who had been in the outer gallery had been chosen to take the answer to Valencia. Since that opportunity was lost, he tells me the plan must be changed again in order to authorize the appointment of members of the Government and that apparently the plan published a few days ago will be selected. This calls for the formation of the committee from deputies and senators who favored the prosecution of the war in Texas, or else the appointment of a certain number of persons who would be acceptable to the leaders.

The revolution has succeeded without the firing of a shot, or a single word's being uttered in condemnation of it. Any foreigner coming into Mexico would not have the slightest idea that the country had gone through an upheaval.

The garrison's plan is being sold on the streets. It consists of the following items:

1. The garrison in the capital is in complete agreement with the plan proclaimed in San Luis Potosí on the 14th of the present month by His Excellency, Don Mariano Paredes y Arrillaga.

2. The same garrison appoints as its commanding officer His Excellency Don Gabriel Valencia, General of Division.

3. The aforesaid plan will be carried out with the additions *which His Excellency, the Commander-in-Chief, is sending to His Excellency, General Don José Joaquin Herrera, in office on this date.*

These *additions* contain the reforms I have previously mentioned. Tornel and Almonte have been commissioned to inform Paredes about the action taken.

Señor Herrera has issued a proclamation vindicating the conduct of his administration, protesting against both plans and announcing that he has sent his resignation to the Chambers because he has not had any help in defending the constitution.

If he had resigned two months ago he still might have been able to save everything.

It is declared that the nomination of the Cabinet members I spoke about before is not assured, but there is no doubt as to the information Reyes gave us this morning on the President's behalf.

Review of yesterday's events and part of today's.

Valencia attended the Council meeting,[70] and many members strongly urged him to put himself at the head of the revolution in order to see that things did not get out of hand. They were afraid of possible disorders in the capital because the inhabitants had been provided with weapons. Furthermore, they distrusted the vague promises made by Paredes in his proclamation. Valencia did not commit himself and resorted to evasive replies.

In the afternoon the man *with the good news*[71] went to the home of *my friend*[72] and asked him if he would decide to declare himself in favor of the revolt, all the while manifesting the greatest indecision himself. *My friend* refused to express a definite opinion, and that was the way matters stood when a messenger came to tell the visitor that he was urgently wanted by some of the leaders, that the revolt was about to break out in the *Ciudadela* and that everything was in the wildest confusion. He left.

The Government, suspecting the loyalty of the commander at the *Ciudadela*,[73] had summoned General Torrejón from Puebla with some troops and had put him in command there. Well, Torrejón did indeed come prepared for the revolution; it was he who rebelled. But since his ability was no match for his bravery[74] everything was soon in the greatest disorder. The disorder had reached its climax when the signal gun was fired. If the Government had been able to rely upon a loyal body of troops and had showed enough energy, the revolt would have been suppressed in five minutes, because among the rebels there was no one who had the qualities of leadership or who had any sense of obedience.

With the continuance of this chaotic state of affairs, it occurred to the rebels to make Valencia their leader. At four o'clock in the morning they went to get him and induce him to accept the command, explaining the situation to him. He decided to accept. Almonte also joined him so that some agreement could be reached as to how to proceed. Later other men who had been called by the leaders arrived, among them five members of the Council. They came to an agreement on what should be done. No

70 By the *Bases Orgánicas,* the Constitution of 1843, a council of seventeen had been established. Valencia was its president.

71 "el de *las buenas noticias.*" Unidentified by the author.

72 Unidentified by the author.

73 i.e., Valencia.

74 The text reads "más como su incapacidad no iguala a su valor," but in Vicente Riva Palacio, *México a través de los siglos* (5 vols., Mexico, 1887-89) IV, 550, it is "más como su capacidad no iguala a su valor." Obviously the former is a misprint and the latter contains the author's real meaning.

deputy or senator attended. Almonte had been working hard. He was Paredes's agent in the city and had been given the job of seeing that the plan was successfully carried out. But Valencia rejected the plan as being too vague and demanded something more definite. Plan after plan was considered, until the compromise I have mentioned was finally adopted, although there were still those who opposed it and wanted only Paredes's original plan. When the final draft was finished it was sent to the Government.

Meanwhile what was going on here was of no little interest. The Colonel of the Fourth Battalion, Don José Uraga,[75] called his officers together at night and urged them as friends and brothers to speak out frankly and honestly. They told him that they sympathized with the rebellion, and he replied that he shared their sentiments. Thereupon they fraternized with the troops in the *Ciudadela,* and the officers came and went without hindrance from the advance guards. This morning when the first suggestions were made to the Government, Uraga sent a letter in which he declared himself on the side of the revolutionists and asked only that the gaps in Paredes's plan be filled, the chief point being that Valencia be named President. He sent two other communications of the same nature. If by this course Uraga thought he could insure the President's personal safety, I shall not be inclined to rebuke him for it.

When the President received the ultimatum he replied that he would take the matter up with the Chambers, and he asked for guarantees of good faith.

General Bustamante communicated with Valencia about nine o'clock in the morning and told him that since the troops no longer had any duties to perform, he would make Valencia responsible for public order. Lieutenant Colonel Castro was the bearer of this message and, some suspicion having been aroused by his mission to the *Ciudadela,* he was summoned by Valencia. The latter asked Castro if he had declared for the revolution or if he were still in sympathy with the Government, to which Castro replied: *"As far as my sympathies go, I am for the revolution. But with respect to my duty I am on the side of the Government as aide to General Bustamante."* Valencia responded by praising him for the sentiments he expressed.

These facts, which I owe to reliable persons who were eyewitnesses, make me believe that General Bustamante did not favor the plan as I had been told. I have found out from these same sources that my mysterious visitor and his companion worked hard to influence Bustamante in an effort to get him to make up his mind to head the rebellion and that he refused, saying that he preferred the unhappiness which would come from seeing himself deserted by his troops.

Tornel, who had been summoned, arrived after the ultimatum had been

75 Colonel José López Uraga had a checkered military career and finally, in 1863, joined the French intervention.

sent to the Government. Since his brother-in-law Bonilla took it into his head to lecture him on his tardiness, an extremely funny scene ensued. Tornel became furious because he had been sent for *after the danger was over* and said he considered this an affront to the badge of office he wore. He said he would remove it and put it in his pocket. He did a great deal of complaining and finally said he was going to leave that instant and join Paredes. It seems, however, that he either did not want to go very badly or that in all his blustering there was a bit of fear, for he kept on saying: *"I am going and I trust that no one will stop me; I believe I am free to go because I have not been considered in this matter . . ."* etc., etc. They said some flattering things to him and as at that moment a message came from Valderas to the effect that the defending troops were to surrender their arms, the whole affair turned out to be a rainbow of peace. Tornel said that it was imperative that Valderas be given a satisfactory reply, and someone thrust a pen into his hand so that he could answer in the manner he thought most proper. The man calmed down then and went on with his duties as secretary, which he preferred in any event.

The events alluded to, and many others that I cannot discuss now, are coming to a climax. For the third time Valencia has moved faster than Paredes; he has changed the latter's plan, and, in my judgment, in quite important details; the two men hate each other. All this means that the seed of discord has been planted today and that seed is fertile.

Valencia has sent an urgent summons to *my friend,* who has asked to be excused. Valencia wants to put him in the Cabinet, and my friend is not especially enthusiastic about the revolution. While I was with him he received word that a meeting had been arranged for this afternoon with my mysterious visitor. He gave me another piece of news that I had been afraid I might hear and which is making me quite nervous. I am being considered for some sort of post. This is the most horrible situation imaginable for an honest man, a man whose sense of honor prompts him to avoid the victors, and whose consideration for the public's welfare prompts him, on the other hand, to believe that he could render good service by cooperating.

The rebel leader has discharged the Professor [Ortiz de Zárate] and has named Don José María Icaza his successor.

The prisoners held by the Government in San Francisco under Balderas were freed at seven o'clock this morning (the 30th); that is, before the ultimatum was sent to the Government.

Valencia has issued a proclamation in which he scores the Government for its apathy, its inclination to deal with the Texans and the indifference manifested by its *useless Cabinet,* and because it *thinks only about protocols* and humiliating treaties. He accuses the Government of failure to live up to the program of the revolution of December 6. "It has betrayed the high hopes of *the sincere liberals* and has looked with insulting scorn upon the humble petitions of the people *regarding the form of government.*" Going from these remarks to a discussion of his own program, he says: "I swear before God and man that I do not now have any other purpose in mind than the noble one of helping the Republic *function in the free manner desired by the people.* Soldiers! You belong to the people because you have come from the ranks of the people. In all cases respect their sovereign will!"

There have been published the remarks addressed by Paredes to his soldiers in an order of the day on the 25th of this month in San Juan del Río, in reply to the manifesto issued in the capital by the President. The following noteworthy passages are found in his speech:

". . . Our enemies are trying in vain to blacken our conduct. In vain do they charge that we are trying to erect *arbitrary power* upon the ruins of liberty. The nation knows that we are marching onward with a purpose that is greater, based on sounder reasons and more definite. The nation knows that it is no longer possible to re-establish *ridiculous or ignominious dictatorships* . . . It is imperative that you tell this to our unfortunate people, *now enslaved by a lawless minority* . . . We are not going to make this a revolution wherein personalities are all-important, nor are we going to repeat *the contemptible farce of a new dictatorship.* We are not going to call a constitutional convention that will sanction *tyranny or the power of a military leader* . . . My ambition is too great to crave power . . . The army, *which represents the wishes of an oppressed people,* has made two promises it is resolved to fulfill: one is *not to contribute in any way to the personal aggrandizement of its leader* . . . We love and defend liberty, but we do not want *the tyranny of the rebels* to be cloaked by its sacred name. We want a *representative* constitution and we shall be the champions of guarantees for the people. We do not, however, want the *permanent anarchy* which is now devouring us. We seek a *strong, stable* power that can protect society; but to govern that society we do not want *either the despotic dictatorship of a soldier or the degrading yoke of the orators.*"

Here are two documents that emanated from what may be considered the same source. They are, however, diametrically opposed in their principles. Today Valencia's language means *federation* and *democracy;* and although he rejects both, it appears that he proposes to flatter the people with his pompous words in order to overcome resistance and create an opportunity for himself. *My friend,* who was present when this document was drawn up, advised him to be a little more explicit, and that in order to provide guarantees for all classes of the people he should add *that it was not his intention to create a despotic, arbitrary power.* Thus no one could think that he entertained ambitions of establishing a military government. Valencia openly remonstrated. On the other hand, Paredes, who boldly flings down the gauntlet to democracy, who does not leave it even the shadow of a hope for the future and who rages against it in his every word, thereby proving that he is at least in favor of the aristocracy, with its pretensions to monarchy, perhaps shows his position more plainly than he ought to in his situation with regard to tyranny and military despotism![76] The contradiction cannot be more obvious and perhaps will produce results more quickly than one might imagine.

We shall soon have our doubts cleared up.

Señor Herrera's resignation contains few words. He mentions the leaders of the revolt, *who have left him no resources with which to offer vigorous opposition.* Because he does not wish his own person to be used as a pretext for the shedding of Mexican blood and because on the other hand defense is impossible, he finds himself obliged to announce to the national Congress that he is giving up the reins of office, *since he cannot and should not resign that* office in favor of any one individual. These remarks meant that he was not resigning in favor of Valencia, who, according to the constitution,[77] was destined for the post since he was President of the Council. But since Valencia had calculated things differently than the President, he was careful to point out in his plan that, with the exception of certain violations of the constitution made in the case of the legislative and personal powers of the chief executive, *the present constitution would continue in force while the new one was being framed.* This maneuver has succeeded in nullifying Paredes's plan and will be the deep-seated cause of bloody misunderstandings that will arise between the two men. This is the third time that the leaders in the capital have forced Paredes out, and the second time that Valencia has done so. It is impossible that Paredes can forgive him.

The following members were the only ones to attend the session of the Chamber of Deputies: Alas, who last year made accusations against S. A. and recently did the same in the case of Paredes, Andrade, Arrioja, Atristaín, Barrea (D. I.), Barrera (P. D.), Boves, Castañares, Duarte, Escandón, Espinosa, Estrada, Flores Alatorre, Flores y Terán, Garay, González Movellán, González de la Vega, Hierro (President), Ibarra, Jiménez, Larrainzair, Madrid, Mora, Moreda, Marentín, Obregón, Portillo, Ochoa Natera, Ortega, Palacios, Pozo Pereda, Rejón, Riva Palacio, Rodríguez de San Miguel, Rojas, Valázquez de la Cadena, Vera, Vertiz, Villanueva, Zamacona. A Deputy told me that the *Pípeles*[78] had been absent. This is the name given to enthusiastic federalists by the opposition party.

Wednesday, the 31st

Tornel and Almonte have returned with bad news. Paredes has rejected the change made in his plan, and now we are all going around shaking hands. It is impossible that he will patiently endure having an adversary as President. When he was told several days ago that Valencia was loyal to the Government, he replied: *"I am glad of that."*

76 Gómez Farías thought that the extremely conservative groups were behind the Paredes revolt. Hutchinson, *Gómez Farías,* 577.

77 The text reads: "las Bases." See footnote Number 14.

78 As Ramírez infers in the next sentence this is more or less a derogatory name for the federalists. Possibly it can be translated as "street walkers."

Tornel and Almonte have left again for Guadalupe[79] with the intention of paving the way for a conference that everyone will attend in order to reach an agreement. In fact, the meeting is going to take place under the most adverse conditions one could imagine; *a magnificent luncheon* has been arranged. Valencia left here at a quarter past ten, accompanied by Vieyra, Sierra y Roso, and an aide. I believe it will be hard for them to agree and equally hard for them not to take leave of one another without a greater mutual hatred. Indeed, it is not at all unlikely that they will come to blows between drinks. There is a story for you.

In '41 the heroes of the reform[80] met in Tacubaya, and in a conference that seemed friendly enough Paredes suddenly burst out into a tirade against Valencia, saying that the latter had come there to meddle, because nobody had invited him and that his services were not required. Valencia pretended to ignore all this and shortly afterward invited Paredes to a luncheon. Paredes made him wait quite a while, and when some of the guests came to tell Paredes that he was the only one who had failed to appear, he started to abuse Valencia in vile language and said that he was ready to insult the man in the worst way he could. *My friend* made him take a more reasonable attitude; but in order to satisfy his own ill humor to some extent, Paredes still kept Valencia waiting for more than an hour. I wonder what Paredes's feelings are now.

Paredes has received word that Salas has been recommended for the post of Commander-in-Chief and apparently is figuring on getting Salas to give up the idea. He has a bitter hatred for Salas, since the latter was the tool S. A. used to humiliate Paredes in 1842. This really can complicate the situation enormously.

Don José María Icaza has been appointed Prefect. The City Council has broken up, and only the Mayor, Reyes Veramendi, remains. The members of the Assembly say that they are going to remain to see what will happen. Perhaps in Veramendi's case his decision was induced by the fact that Señor Herrera ignored him during the time troops were being enlisted for the defense of the city.

The foregoing brings to mind an incident told me by certain trustworthy persons. They say that on the day the Government was empowered to take prisoners, Dr. Iturralde had a conference with Señor Herrera in which he expressed his regret at seeing the President in such a cruel predicament and offered his personal and financial assistance. Señor Herrera replied, with a singular lack of tact, that he had absolutely no need of such services and that wherever there was negligence in carrying out the Government's power to take prisoners, Iturralde was to exert

79 Village on the outskirts of Mexico City where the shrine of Guadalupe is located.
80 Apparently this is a reference to the revolt against Bustamante in which Santa Anna, Paredes, and Valencia were involved and from which Santa Anna emerged triumphant.

himself to the utmost. Other similar incidents are being discussed, and as a result I have noted that quite a few individuals have been discouraged from visiting Herrera in his present awkward situation. Perhaps despondency and illness have brought him to this pass, or it may be that the whole story is exaggerated.

Paredes's troops began to enter the city at half-past five this afternoon. They say that the whole force will be here within three days to make a show of their numbers and thus persuade the people that resistance would be futile. The troops who came in belong to the light infantry, which left yesterday with Ampudia at their head. The story of these troops is curious. Ampudia and the officers at the *Ciudadela* agreed to support the rebellion. Last night, therefore, he marched his troops out to join those at the *Ciudadela*. But bewildered and alarmed by what was happening, he decided to join Paredes and actually did leave the city. When he got to the highway[81] he heard the shot of the signal gun from the *Ciudadela* but did not dare return. It was due to this strange chance that he was not the leader of the insurrection and that his place was taken by Valencia, who assumed control of the revolution. Such was the chaotic state of affairs in which these things took place.

At a quarter after four the six cannon that had been put into position at the President's Palace were removed to the *Ciudadela*. The crowds hurried to get a closer view and to march along with the instruments of their enslavement, which were misrepresented as the faithful instruments of their sovereign will.[82]

Civil war has broken out among the Carmelites. Their present Provincial, who has been in office for eighteen years, wants to retain control, but since he does not have the support of the Mexicans in the order, it is said that he has summoned forty lay brothers to come from Spain, where they espoused the cause of Don Carlos, and has asked them to bring recruits. The person who published this news in the *Siglo* calls attention to the Monarchist propaganda that they might undertake to spread, relying upon a Bourbon party within the country. Father Nájera is the target of the friars' resentment.

The *Siglo XIX* announces that its editors are *withdrawing from a conflict in which their ideals find no cause for further struggle*, now that the revolution has triumphed. This is the fourth time that this insignificant and cowardly sheet has run away. All that it knows how to do is to kick a man when he is down.[83] It is without any program or principles other than making money and, through people's fears of defamation and libel,

81   Probably the Tacubaya highway.
82   The text reads: "los instrumentos de su esclavidad y fieles órganos de su soberana voluntad," but in Riva Palacio, *México a través de los siglos*, IV, 551, "los instrumentos de su esclavitud, *disfrazados de fieles órganos de su soberana voluntad.*"
83   The text reads: "a toro muerto gran lanzada." Literally, "a big sword-thrust into a dead bull."

gaining for its editors a certain political influence. It has done an immense amount of harm by confusing public opinion without furnishing adequate information and by encouraging anarchy. God grant that its demise may be a certainty this time!

Everything was ready tonight at the Cathedral for the great celebration held every year, but since there was no President to render thanks to God for the happy termination of the year, the people left. They were disappointed because they had been looking for amusement. This intended tribute occasioned by fear of Paredes must not have been gratifying to Valencia, who was acting constitutional President. Aside from this, everything turned out all right, since there was no necessity for giving thanks for the political situation, although there was a reason for giving thanks for the benefits that Providence has reserved for us in this defeat. I make these statements because the proverb, "It's an ill wind that blows nobody any good," is in my opinion proved.

Valencia has returned from Guadalupe, and although up to the present time (ten o'clock at night) nothing positive has been learned about the plan which definitely will prevail, I have been reliably informed that the situation is assuming an absolutely new aspect. Valencia has given way before Paredes's opposition and states that he is satisfied with the results of the conference. A friend tells me that these two rivals have never before been as closely united. This is probably the reason why events could not have transpired otherwise. I doubt, however, that the deal will be sincere and lasting.

The year has ended with the revolution's bringing a new and fertile source of future troubles. Since in my notes I have written under the melancholy inspiration dictated by events, the profound sentiments I have experienced have induced me to express myself in harsh words and humiliating terms directed against our people. They are more worthy of pity than of censure, because no one can be expected to do what he has not been taught to do, nor to be different from what he is. Republican institutions, based on the system of representation, demand such a great pooling of individual knowledge that perhaps none of the most cultured nations of Europe possesses sufficient skill to make the system work; the system can thrive only if it is nourished by customs which themselves are the products of toil and industry, stimulated by institutions that have attained the power to develop as they have in the United States. We lack both these elements; but on the other hand, we have a people that are the most docile and humble in the whole world, a people who have the least physical and spiritual requirements: in other words, a people who are the easiest to govern. As long as our institutions are not adapted to the people's character and general moral make-up with which the Creator has endowed them, we must avoid both the anarchy of half-hearted efforts and the despotism of military men, until Europe, tired of our vacillation, imposes upon us the yoke of a foreign monarchy. Our institutions will have a firm foundation only if they follow the dictum of Tacitus: *Nec totam libertatem, nec totam servitutem!*[84]

From the 27th to the 30th
Supplement

Ampudia has been the motivating force of the revolution in the capital. He sent Betancourt to withdraw the battalion from Celaya and he ought to have been proclaimed General-in-Chief at the *Ciudadela*. Confused and frightened by what was happening, however, Ampudia believed the cause was lost and left with the light infantry for the guard post at Vallejo.[85] The troops stationed there joined him, and taking their one cannon, they all started out to join Paredes, as I mentioned in the events of December 31. By his actions, so some of the officers say, Ampudia *compromised both his life and his honor.* All this has caused Valencia a great deal of annoyance, since people are calling him a meddler because they say he snatched the glory and position away from the leader who took the risks. Here is another source of military anarchy.

The 30th

The churchmen at Guadalupe were expecting Paredes and were in the midst of preparations for a great celebration, including, as was natural, the customary *Te Deum.* Valencia arrived and since the announcement merely said that *the General* had come, the good fathers, who did not make any distinctions between political personages, ordered the church bells to be rung as they prepared for the august ceremony. At this point fickle Destiny entered with her worries and tribulations. Would Valencia accept the honors? If he did Paredes would be furious at such a brazen usurpation of his prerogatives. Would he refuse the honors? If he did it would mean humiliation for him, who was in fact the one exercising supreme authority. What was there to do in this exceedingly difficult situation? Valencia hit upon an admirable way out of the dilemma, a way that revealed his obvious talents in such emergencies, and thereby proved that he is not the commonplace type of individual so many people think he is. He went to the Dean of the Cathedral and told him to have just a simple Hail Mary sung.

The 31st

The *Voz del Pueblo*[86] has come to the end of its career. In the serious accusations it makes against the defeated party one can discern indications of its secret scorn for the victorious revolution, which the editors have not dared to criticize openly. I have always thought that the sympathies of this paper were fundamentally liberal, even though it has warmly defended the interests of S. A. and of the army. This was merely its foolish

84   Neither too much liberty nor too much servitude.
85   Guard post on the outskirts of Mexico City near Guadalupe.
86   *The Voice of the People*, a newspaper in Mexico City.

way of obtaining its objectives, since its editors believed that under the protection of both these sides the federalist cause would triumph. Wretched enthusiasts who are always trying to make the ravings of their imaginations absolute realities! The *Voz del Pueblo* was one of the staunchest supporters of the revolution, because it aroused the hatred of the soldiers against the civil power and strengthened the soldiers' ideas of their own importance and privileges. In short, it helped the revolution because it made the soldiers consider the Government a constant threat to their existence and to their special privileges; it cut the army off from society by urging it into open warfare against the people. Its editors were fitted for the dismal job that they had undertaken. The top editor (Augustín Franco) is a young man who not only writes with a fiery pen and with good style but also has the fanatical conscience of a tribune.[87]   His collaborator (Anastasio Cerecero) who is gifted with no less talent, wrote with the cold calculation of an ambitious man without means or reputation, an individual whom society has scornfully rejected. This is an example of how two characters so diametrically opposite can come together on common ground in order to create an immense evil when circumstances give them an opportunity. These circumstances were unfortunately made just right for them by the blunders of the weak, sluggish Government they were fighting, a Government so stolid that it was not able to understand the influence of the press and made a big show of ignoring it. On one occasion when Couto was particularly annoyed by the remarks of Rodríguez, who was trying without much success to explain to him the harm that the opposition papers were causing in the capital and the various departments, he remarked, "*No one pays any attention to what they say, and I myself never bother to read those sheets.*" The Minister adhered to this attitude so consistently that he ordered the editor of the *Diario* to suppress the editorials! The *Voz del Pueblo* is thus reaping the harvest of its indiscreet preaching. For the second time the federalists have created a military power in order to bring about the triumph of their utopian schemes, and the trail left by this power will be marked on our map of today the same way the ancient Mexicans marked on their map, now in the Museum, the trail left by the Chichimecas[88] when they invaded the country; that is to say, *with a broad line of blood.*

The *Monitor Constitucional*[89] has also suffered. Its editor (García Torres) is now an exile because of the last article he wrote criticizing the revolution.

Supplement
The 29th

The Archbishop of Oaxaca[90] told me the following story: An officer entered his house and asked for the adobe bricks that formed the borders

87 A magistrate in Roman government.
88 Indian tribe of northern Mexico.
89 Newspaper in Mexico City.
90 Oaxaca is both a city and state in southeastern Mexico.

of the flower beds in the garden, explaining that he wanted them for use in constructing a barricade nearby. The Archbishop became angry at this, but like a sensible man who knows where the shoe pinches, he restrained himself, and after a moment of reflection said: *"If I refuse you will take them anyway, just as if I had given them to you, so go ahead and take as many as you wish."* The officer answered him in the same natural, frank manner he would employ in speaking about any other commonplace matter: "This won't be the first time, you know. About this time last year I took your adobe bricks to build a barricade against General S. A. (we were on General Paredes's side). I gave you a receipt for them so that the Government could repay you. Do you want me to give you another receipt for these that I am going to take now?" What can one expect from a politico-military conscience like this?

The 31st

My friend told me that Pedraza went into hiding at Tanepantla; perhaps he thought that the best way to escape Paredes's search for him was to hide in one of the places along the route Paredes was taking. Of course, Paredes, who was in Tanepantla, heard about it immediately through the military commandant and sent word to Pedraza that there was no need for him to keep on hiding. He advised him to either come out and show himself or else to return to Mexico City with complete assurance of his safety, because no one was going to persecute him. The Archbishop of Oaxaca told me that Paredes had informed the Archbishop of Mexico City that no one had any cause for alarm and that all those who had gone into hiding could come forth, since he was not coming to persecute anyone.

The 30th

Valencia did not want to take part in the insurrection; but at last, after he had been urged to do so by his friends, he promised. He agreed, however, only on the condition that Torrejón, in command at the *Ciudadela*, would support the rebels also. Since he was afraid that something might go wrong he demanded as a guarantee and a signal that a shot be fired from the gun at the *Ciudadela*. The signal was therefore intended especially for him.

The 27th

Adjutant Don Joaquín G. Granados was ordered by the Government to inform Paredes about the decree of the Congress requiring that all rebels lay down their arms under penalty of certain reprisals. Paredes and his army were given forty-eight hours to comply. Granados tells me that today he found Paredes on the march at a place beyond San Juan del Río, and that as soon as the latter was informed about the decree he commanded his men to halt. He ordered *the decree read to all the troops so that they might realize that they had a perfect right to decide for them-*

selves, now that they were apprised of the real situation. This master stroke produced the calculated results, for the troops answered with cheers for the army and their chief and with cries of "Down with the civilian authorities!"[91] General Don Simeón Ramírez said to Paredes: "Tell the Government and the Congress to go straight to hell[92] and shoot these men (the emissaries) as a good beginning." These coarse words are a true reflection of the sentiments of the army toward the civil authority. They also give quite a precise estimate of our social conditions. Paredes treated Granados well and even had him ride with him in his carriage.

The——[93]

The preliminary meeting of the deputies has given indications of partiality and shamelessness, which indicates that little can be expected of it in the future; it has just deprived our Congresses of what little reputation they had left. The press had denounced the election of Otero as illegal because he was not of the required age. However, he ignored the charges and did not present his resignation because he thought he was complying with the dictates of his duty and his sense of decency by maintaining silence about his age. "If they ask me my age," he said, "I'll tell it. And if they don't I shall take my seat in the Chamber." Here is a rare bit of moral rectitude quite worthy of a distinguished place in the *Cartas Provinciales!* There was quite a bit of opposition to Otero in the Chamber, and so the Rules Committee[94] questioned him about his age. When he replied that he was not old enough, the committee decided not to approve his credentials. A long, scandalous debate ensued on this point, Otero's supporters claiming that the *proof*, based on his own words, should be disregarded in favor of the *presumption*, supplied by the Electoral College. This business needs no comment. The fact is that the decision to refuse his credentials was voted down, twenty-nine to twenty-eight, and when the question was put to a special vote on the basis of its merits it was approved by the same margin. Otero bravely and with good conscience came in and took his seat. Now let us get on with this! This record was read at the following session, and when the names of those voting were called, *three* deputies complained that someone had used their names to vote against the proposal for rejection and for the approval of Otero's credentials. Their argument was unanswerable: *they had not been present at the session.* After these remarks it was clear that there had been a substitution of votes and that the credentials legally had been rejected. Then the Otero partisans resorted to another bit of foolishness in order to get out of the difficulty. Following the procedure used on such occasions, they asked *whether the decision was approved with the corrections indicated by the three members who had complained,* and with his credentials

91 The text reads: "y con mueras a los cívicos."
92 The text reads: ". . . que vayan al c——."
93 The text reads: "Día . . ."
94 "Comisión de poderes."

thus approved, Otero was considered authorized to continue as a member. But his credentials had really been rejected by a vote of twenty-eight to twenty-six.

On the 28th Otero displayed his shameless attitude before our Chamber as a member of the committee in charge of delivering the message[95] that the Congress was installed. A Chamber that so brazenly flouted the law and all decency in matters as fundamental as this one could not inspire confidence or respect. And what shall we say about the man who took such pride in these disgraceful proceedings? Otero has done the nation all the harm within his power. But it was not through his own efforts that he was able to do this, and he will go on in his career, thanks to the political and moral ineptitude of his countrymen. In any other country he could not even appear in public without running the risk of being put to shame. But in our country he occupies a certain position of respect and he almost succeeded in getting the post of Minister of Foreign Affairs in the vacillating administration of Señor Herrera. The Plan of Tacubaya gave Otero the start on his political career and he sided with General Paredes at Guadalajara in opposing the city's demand for federation. These opinions served to get him an appointment as a member of the Council of Representatives which was set up by Santa Anna. His position here was ambiguous but it enabled him to influence the Cabinet to appoint him as a deputy to the 1842 Congress when it annulled the Guadalajara election. Bocanegra, then Minister of Foreign Affairs, has told me that the list of appointees was approved in his office. Through Cumplido, who was connected with *Siglo XIX*, Otero became closely associated with Don Juan Batista Morales (the Pythagorean Cock) and his position as a deputy being assured, he began to show signs of federalist sympathies. At the instigation of Pedraza and Rodríguez Puebla he was appointed to the commission for the study of the constitution. There he listened passively to the discussion until the majority had agreed upon a plan, at which time he took a separate stand to urge a special vote, thus centering attention on himself, and openly proposed federation. When he had thus attained his goal of setting himself apart from the others, he immediately about-faced and withdrew his vote on the day the majority proposal was voted down, and a week later without difficulty signed an entirely different plan.[96] Gifted with a great facility in speaking and surrounded by others who were mediocre, he thought he was one of the greatest orators of the century. His flair for talking so carried him away that two or three times he was seen to rise from his seat in order to talk *against* a proposal, and then finding that the allotted number of speeches in opposition had already been scheduled, he spoke *in favor* of the measure. By cleverly playing upon the nation's hatred of S. A. and by rushing into print with democratic ideas

95   To the President.
96   This apparently is a reference to the Congress of 1842 and its attempt to formulate a new constitution, which it failed to do.

of the most exaggerated sort, he kept up his efforts to win popular support in preparation for his return to his seat in the Chambers, for this was his fondest dream. When the constitution[97] was put into effect it immediately barred his way, as it did in the case of Lafragua[98] and other enthusiastic democrats, by raising the age limit. In this manner he was excluded from the Congress of 1844. In the meantime he was the object of a certain amount of persecution, which led to his being exiled, but this was more than offset by the popularity he gained. *Siglo XIX* carried on a war to the death against the constitution and against S. A. until the latter fell from power in December of that year. At that time there was to be an election of a new municipal government. Moved by his passion for parliaments as well as by his determination to assure his political future, Otero agreed to an election plot that made it easy for him to take over the office of mayor. While the disturbances resulting from the insurrection on the 6th[99] were still going on, the so-called "liberal" electors came together and agreed to call a meeting, on a fixed day, of only as many of the other electors as was needed for a quorum; the remaining electors would not be notified in time; that is, only after the session had been adjourned. They carried out their plan and by this method succeeded in converting their own minority into a majority, thereby getting the kind of election which pleased them. This occurrence gave rise to such dissatisfaction that Riva Palacio, who was Minister at that time, tried to annul the election and was restrained from doing so only at the instance of Echevarría.[100] Otero therefore became a member of the municipal governing board; in just about the same way he recently secured his seat in the Chamber of Deputies. The Assembly was shocked at these developments and rushed through a decree declaring that only citizens of Mexico City could become members of the city government.

The leaders of the insurrection on the 6th of December decided to give the movement a completely legal status; that is, they wanted to continue the observance of the existing constitution and to put aside any consideration of a federation. Otero, seeing an opportunity to start his career anew, joined these men. As a result, *Siglo XIX* began to attack the plan for federation and those who were defending it. When Otero persisted in his attitude he ran up against opposition on the part of his friends in the municipal government by refusing to sign a petition which they had drawn up requesting federation. Two opposing groups sprang up, and Otero's popularity suffered a severe blow. *Siglo XIX* and its partisans were nicknamed "Sunflowers," and the fight went on, with Otero maintaining *an attitude of uncertainty*. What Otero lost on this side he gained on the side of the Government, which gave him reason to hope for a post in the

97 Constitution of 1843, known as "las Bases."
98 José M. Lafragua was a liberal and a good friend of Gómez Farías.
99 December 6, 1844.
100 Pedro Echevarría was also a member of the Cabinet.

Cabinet. This hope kept him in sympathy with the Government, and that is why *Siglo XIX* suppressed the bad features and praised the good ones in the Government's long and blundering career. The federalists on the *Voz del Pueblo,* and the partisans of Santa [Anna][101] on the *Amigo del Pueblo,*[102] who likewise were defending federation, cast a dismal shadow over him. But he could not get a start in his chosen field of endeavors because of the obstacles that the Government put in his way. The above-mentioned newspapers humiliated him by portraying him as obstinate and finally said and did so many things against him that ultimately the *Siglo* also went into the federalist camp. For this reason the young physician, Navarro, was added to the editorial staff. He was a fanatical democrat who was not in the habit of handling anybody with kid gloves and he fought each and every economic and political principle that the *Siglo* had espoused in previous years. When he was criticized for his inconsistency in behavior he replied that the editors of the *Siglo* were not always the same and that each had his own personal ideas and wrote according to his own convictions. In this way Otero got an additional black mark against him but he continued to keep on good terms with the Government in the hope of obtaining the post of Minister. He was already on the point of sounding out the Government on this matter when he received a disappointment in the very field of activity where he had made his previous mistakes. After he had been appointed defense attorney for the official who . . .[103]

101 Inserted by editor.
102 *Friend of the People,* a newspaper in Mexico City.
103 Here Genaro García notes that the narrative comes to an end.

CHAPTER II

THE REVOLUTION AND GOVERNMENT OF PAREDES

Thursday, the 1st[1]

Although there has been a great deal of news about the new political order in the offing, nothing certain is known about it. *My friend* told me this morning that the only sure thing is the perfect harmony between Valencia and Paredes, because the former has made concessions or, rather, disavowed what he had previously done. The Administration's program is to be agreed upon at Guadalupe. It will be made public here, but not until after a Council meeting of sixty individuals who will have the job of settling the Administration's future policies. Before they do this they are waiting for a proclamation by the capital garrison, a proclamation which will indicate its humble adherence to the plan of Paredes. He is due to enter the city on Saturday, the 3rd.

I have learned through this same source that Valencia is governing as President of the Council, and in this capacity has taken some rather bold steps. He has dismissed González Ángulo from his job as Director of the Mint and has reinstated Cacho in his place. I have heard some severe criticism about this business. It is said that he has even promoted some military men as a reward for recent service.

I went to the home of *my friend* to forestall a serious calamity which is threatening me, if I can believe, as I must, the news that two other trustworthy friends of mine have brought me. They have told me that I have been put on the list of Council members. This is a true misfortune; a horrible event in the stormy history of my life. In the town where my family lives, where my interests and affections have always been, there are low-minded conscienceless men who envy me. They would not view in the proper light my refusal of an office and would use it as a pretext to justify their uncalled-for hatred of me. I suspect that my participation would lighten for them the slavery which threatens us all, because A[lmonte] who at present is the most trusted adviser of Paredes, thinks very highly of me and will insist on working me in on the new order of things. But I repeat that those scoundrels would persecute me relentlessly and turn any good I could do for them into evil. In order to avoid any such misfortune I went to see *my friend* to get him to use his influence with Valencia so that I might escape this cruel predicament. Valencia has been quite friendly with him. At a quarter past three I left *my friend's* home because he had just received word that Valencia was going to pay him a visit. I met the latter on the stairway and although he embraced me and shook my hand, it seemed to me that he was not particularly eager for me to remain. He looked as if he were worried about something. I wonder what it could have been?

1 January, 1846.

Everything has changed this afternoon! . . . The airs that Valencia has been putting on in his capacity of President and the things he has been doing have produced a terrific explosion. The leaders of the revolt, who are by no means on friendly terms with him, together with a great many other influential people, who likewise do not think much of him, have brought events to a head. Indeed, Paredes himself may be the prime mover in all this. He saw that his rival had taken a place at the table and was all ready to occupy the seat of honor at the banquet that had been spread before him. A bold and energetic blow that left everybody astounded stopped him in the midst of his headlong career. An abrupt command which some among those present toned down a bit in its harshness and peremptory character unexpectedly put Valencia on the sidelines. In this command Paredes indicated that he himself was to be officially recognized as the one and only leader with sole authority, and that everything was to be put in order for his reception in the city on the following day. At that time he would call a Council meeting *at which he himself would preside* to draw up a definite revolutionary program.

Valencia was like a man thunderstruck, and in his first display of anger spoke about crushing Paredes and fortifying himself in the city to resist him, counting upon the great influence he thought he had among the troops of the garrison and also in the army. He was bitterly disappointed because the garrison had already announced its unequivocal sympathy for Paredes's plan and had recognized him as its leader. Should anything happen to Paredes, Almonte was to take his place. The proclamation further stated that the garrison would never support either Valencia or Tornel, who were said to be interlopers. The charge, however, was couched in mild terms. As soon as Paredes received the declaration of the garrison, he issued the order that I have spoken about. Valencia immediately withdrew to his home and sent Paredes an avowal of his submission. He added that if his presence was an obstacle he would ask for a passport enabling him to live for a couple of years outside the Republic. Paredes scornfully read this statement and said that he did not consider Valencia or anybody else capable of frightening him. "I come," he said, "resolved to make my ideas triumph or to perish in the attempt. Although I have made up my mind not to persecute anyone for his previous deeds, I shall shoot anyone who now gets in my way, whether he be an archbishop, a general, a magistrate, or anyone else." Everyone believes that he is capable of doing what he says, and for this reason he is looked upon with fear and terror.

Valencia's misfortune has wrecked all my plans to save myself, for I do not have the slightest influence with Paredes. He is quite capable of making an example of the first man who refuses to discharge the duties of the position designated for him· How much embarrassment and grief have been caused me by this accursed business that brought me to Mexico City! And to think that I cannot give it up!

Siglo XIX has appeared again under the name *Memorial histórico* to guarantee its right to be cowardly and so that it will not become an insolvent enterprise. The *Monitor* is making a big effort to get subscribers and to take the place of *Siglo XIX*. This is the formidable Power of the Press for you! *Auri sacra fames.*[2]

Friday, the 2nd

Very early today posters were put up on all the street corners. They read as follows: "Announcement to the People. Today His Excellency Don Mariano Paredes y Arrillaga will enter the Capital with the army under his command. The citizens are hereby urged to decorate their houses and in this way demonstrate the dictates of their patriotism." A short time later these posters were either torn to pieces or scribbled on with obscene words. When the rebels saw that patriotism would not succeed in getting even one bit of bunting hung up for decoration, they sent out soldiers a short time before the troops were to enter the city, and these soldiers warned the citizens who lived on the streets along which the troops were to pass that balconies were to be properly hung with bunting. This was done. But it was the only display of bunting that Señor Paredes saw on his passage through the city. There was not a single bit of bunting on the main square, except for the *official* decorations on the City Hall and the President's Palace.

The officer second in command on the general staff went to receive Paredes on the outskirts of the city, taking with him the troops of the garrison, probably to swell the numbers and increase the fears of the citizens. Paredes was greatly put out because the commanding general himself [Salas] had not met him in person and burst out into violent words, even insulting the officer. Valencia stayed in his house. I have been assured that during the first talks between the leaders of the invading troops and the commanders of the local garrison some in the group would ask whether, after all, the recall of General S. A. was not being considered.

In order to make the entrance of the army more impressive and solemn, the troops were ordered to march along the Calle de Donceles and then the streets in the San Francisco quarter with General Paredes, surrounded by his aides, at their head. At seventeen minutes to one the troops entered the plaza by the Mercaderes gate. Six minutes later, General Paredes entered the plaza on horseback. He wore his full dress uniform and looked about him with such self-possesion that one could not determine whether his attitude was one of pride or scorn. He followed the column of troops and rode in front of the Palace without even glancing at the people who jammed the balconies. He remained in the plaza about a quarter of an hour, and then went to the Post Office building where his family had been living since the time he was named Collector of Revenue by S. A. This peculiar behavior of his has made a profound impression on the public. The

2 Gold has a sacred reputation.

second column of troops was the famous Fourth Battalion under the command of Colonel Uraga. They carried the flag given to them in June by Señor Herrera. It bore a motto in letters of gold which commemorated the fact that the Battalion had saved the constitutional cause on June 7.[3] Tonight there is to be a meeting at the Palace composed of the generals and other leaders who have been charged with carrying out the law; or rather, as General Paredes said in his proclamation today: "charged with the duty of amending the political principles adopted at San Luis, in order to fill the vacuum which it was necessary to leave *out of respect for public opinion and out of due consideration for the people's rights* and to indicate that there are certain obligations to be fulfilled on behalf of the people." These phrases have been criticized but no explanation of them has been forthcoming. As a result, it has been quite logically deduced that *respect for public opinion and consideration for the rights of the people* would be destroyed by the explanation to be given by the generals and the leaders.

Valencia told *my friend* that Paredes had requested a conference with him and had sent word to him that *conversation brings about an understanding between peoples.* He added other similar expressions. Nevertheless, judging by what P—[4] has told me, I suspect that if Paredes requested a meeting with Valencia it was only to oblige the latter to agree with his plans and to sense the full power of his authority. Paredes was in conference behind closed doors with Tornel, Almonte, Gutiérrez, and . . .[5] in which he reviewed his plans. In the meantime he made Valencia wait a long time in the anteroom.

P— was with Valencia when Almonte came out of the conference, and when he went over to Valencia and greeted him cordially, the latter replied in a cold, haughty manner. Turning to P— Valencia said: "Look at that black-hearted scoundrel just out of the conference and the airs he's putting on. Why, I was ready to retire when he had just started on his career." It is not likely to be forgotten that only about a month and a half before this there was a secret, cordial reconciliation between the two leaders.

The *Army's General Manifesto,* which is to be the basis of our constitution, has been issued. This manifesto is a second edition of the Plan of Tacubaya revised and enlarged, and also a facsimile of the decree of November 29, 1846,[6] which put the sword into Paredes's hand for the purpose of striking down S. A. In Article One the legislative and executive powers are declared deposed *because they did not fulfill the desires and requirements of the nation, they did not maintain the dignity of its name and they did not try to preserve the integrity of its territory.* In Articles Two and Three arrangements are made for a meeting of a council of representatives from

3   1845.
4   Pedraza?
5   Per text.
6   Should read "1844."

the various departments to be appointed by Paredes for the sole purpose of electing an interim President, who will be in charge while the special Congress is assembling, and of receiving the usual oath of allegiance from him, after which the council will cease to function. Article Four declares that the powers of the President *are derived from the laws now in force,* and that he can go *beyond them* only for the purpose of preparing the national defense, *always preserving the guarantees provided by the law.* Article Five fixes the responsibility of the ministers with relation to the first constitutional Congress, *but states that their acts are at no time subject to revision.* Article Six authorizes the President to issue a call for the new Congress within a week, and this Congress is to meet some time within the next four months in the capital of the Republic, under the proviso that *in issuing its new constitution it will not tamper with nor alter the principles or guarantees which the Republic adopted during the previous regime.* Article Seven deals with the continuation of the Council. Article Eight requires the resignation of all department authorities who oppose the plan, *others to be appointed in their place in conformity with the laws governing their appointment.* Article Nine preserves the powers of the Judiciary. Article Ten guarantees that *no one shall be persecuted because of his previous political views.* This act was approved by all those present with the exception of General Don Lino José Alcorta, who stated that he considered the points decided upon as within the province of the legislative authority and that he was only a soldier whose duty was to obey. General Don José Vicente Miñón said that he had remained loyal to the Government up until the final day and for that reason he, too, could not give his approval to the plan agreed upon. This noble, firm stand of his almost caused dismay, but no one was sufficiently resolute to do likewise. Among those who signed the act were Generals Don Ignacio Ormaechea, Don José G. de la Cortina and Don Melchor Álvarez, senators in the outgoing Congress; Don Isidro Reyes, senator in both the outgoing and the new Congress; and Don Nicolás Bravo, Don Vicente Filisola, and Don Juan N. Almonte, senators in the new Congress. Don Luis G. Vieyra and Don Ignacio Ormaechea y Ernaín were among the deputies who signed. General Don Anastasio Bustamante did not attend, although he was summoned. It is said, however, that he expressed his willingness to abide by the decision of the majority. This fact needs confirmation. Bravo was the second to sign, followed by Valencia.

Saturday, the 3rd

P—, who had had a very long and interesting conference with Paredes, sent me an urgent call to meet him at nine o'clock in the morning. I found him quite enthusiastic over the repeated assurances Paredes had given him as to his good intentions and his desire to consult with persons able to advise him about the proper steps to take for the welfare and prosperity of the nation. When P— spoke to me about this matter neither of us had as yet seen the *Army's General Manifesto.* We had to wait for this until half-past four in the afternoon, when it was printed and distributed. Meanwhile, the people had been kept in an inexpressible state of anxiety. P—'s lengthy eulogy ended with a suggestion that overwhelmed me: he wanted to take me to see Paredes! I immediately remonstrated both because I had made up my mind never to take part in politics again and especially because I had had no dealings of any kind with Paredes and barely know him.

P—'s enthusiasm for the general welfare of the people kept him from understanding my reluctance, because he thought it quite natural for a man in Paredes's position to be surrounded by all kinds of individuals and did not take into account any ceremoniousness dictated by good taste. But since I had adopted the policy of never going to meet important personages, a policy I have never abandoned, I found myself compelled to cause him several moments of embarrassment, in spite of the fact that his arguments were having some effect on me.

These arguments, in fact, were quite just and well-founded, since he informed me that the man had fallen into the clutches of that crowd of miserable parasites who have corrupted the nation and reduced it to despair, and as a consequence he was eager to have honest men around him, men who could guide him and point out the proper course to take. Then P— went on to explain what we could expect if those parasites ever succeeded in getting the upper hand; honest men who had refused to cooperate would be responsible for such a situation. I have always been gullible when it came to arguments like these, and as a result of this weakness I have been plunged into not a few political schemes that have brought me untold grief and woe. I felt myself about to give in, but the thought that I was to be the one to cultivate the friendship when he had just expelled me from Congress gave me strength, and after four hours of discussion I resolutely refused to visit the man.

In our country there is what I believe to be a thoroughly regrettable attitude, because I have seen its opposite in the history of all other nations and in concepts which are the products of more rational thinking. In times of political unrest the defeated party does not, and can never hope to, aspire to anything except freedom from persecution by the victors. If in defeat the losers can succeed in guaranteeing the preservation of even a few remnants of the principles for which they have fought, their defeat is not conclusive, and as time goes by they can consider themselves on the way to realizing their hopes. This state of affairs is so natural that there has always been a secret struggle between victors and vanquished to get their candidates into the new administration. It is like a life-and-death contest. In our unusual nation, however, exactly the reverse is true. Here at the very time that the defeated party cries to heaven against the tyranny and intolerance of its opponents, accusing them of having seized all the jobs, it criticizes and expels any of its own candidates who accepts a post from the victors and persecutes him as it would a renegade! I cannot understand the temperament of my people nor can I analyze the motives that prompt them to such actions. If it were not for this type of thinking that governs the country's behavior I would accept a post in this administration, because the iron-like will and the thorough honesty of General Paredes are characteristics that I would require of any government I happened to serve. I would not take any job without them. However, this business would finally ruin me. Let those who have gone over to the new Government suffer the consequences of their fickleness.

P— returned this afternoon quite distressed. He complains, and rightly so, about the unwise severity with which Article One of the *Manifesto* has been drawn up. It gives no opportunity for an honorable man to accept a seat in the Council if he has served in the old Congress, since if he did accept it would be tantamount to confessing that he deserves the criticism he gets in the new session. God keep me from this sort of disgrace!

The Council has met in unaccustomed haste. The man[7] is clever and bold in his planning, thereby assuring himself of success in realizing his twin goals: impressing the people and getting what he is after. He summoned the members of the Council an hour before the stipulated meeting time and along with his summons he managed to draw up a number of ordinances. The respect which he inspires is proved by the fact that almost all the Council members arrived for the meeting at the appointed time. Such a thing as this has never been seen before in the case of our governing bodies. *Forty-three* members attended, with only three absent. The Council proceeded to the election of a President, and although rumor had it that the choice would fall upon Almonte, Paredes was elected *unanimously*.

The people, who never could quite understand what was going on, were to experience the same shocking surprise that I experienced when *at half-past ten at night* they heard cannon shots in the central plaza, followed by the ringing of the alarm bells in the Cathedral. I was frozen to the spot, not knowing the reason for all this extraordinary excitement. My consternation was such that I could explain the occurrence only by another that might be similar: I fancied that a revolt had taken place in the President's Palace and that Paredes must have been shot.

Anecdotes

At the Council of Generals on the second of the month, Requena, who was defending Rangel,[8] proposed that an order be issued setting him at liberty, since the plan stated that no one would be persecuted for his previous views. Paredes replied that in this case it was not a question of opinions, but of a prison sentence that was being carried out, and that

7 Paredes.
8 General Joaquín Rangel was a supporter of Santa Anna. In an unsuccessful coup in 1845 he had captured President Herrera, but the latter's followers arrived in time to save him. As a result Rangel had been sentenced to ten years in prison.

he did not come to nullify the results of such sentences. Someone else ventured to suggest the same leniency with regard to S. A. Paredes told Gordoa that he had all possible guarantees that the General would not decide to set foot on the soil of the Republic. The first of my predictions has come true. Perhaps the others will not.

Everyone believes it to be a foregone conclusion that Tornel will be Minister of War, and he himself considers the appointment as a certainty. Basing his remarks on these circumstances, he told *my friend,* with that nonchalant, jesting air of his that makes people forget even his bad qualities: "If I am offered the post of Minister, I shall accept it; but only on three conditions, the first of which is *that I shall not be obliged to sign any dispatches,*" etc. This type of activity has been his main weakness. It has fattened his purse while impoverishing the country, and has secured a sizable clientele for him. That particular incident, cruel joke that it was, can be matched by another which occurred one day when he was regretting the bitter criticism heaped upon him by certain individuals. He said: "*The Nation has the right to complain about me, and about me alone.*" I know that for precisely this reason Paredes has been hesitating to give him the appointment. But who knows whether Paredes will have the courage to disappoint him in view of the fact that Tornel was so valuable in helping him plan the revolt? If Paredes does ignore him, it will cause general consternation.

While Valencia was engaged in conversation with three of his friends concerning the appointment of members of the council of Representatives, one of them remarked that Valencia and several others he mentioned would certainly be among the number. Valencia replied: "No, because since Bravo, Almonte, and I shall be candidates for the Presidency it will not be proper for us to be members of the Council." Valencia has received the final, painful blow which must have hurt his pride severely, for Paredes left him out and appointed the other two as his *co-candidates.*

A few moments after Paredes was elected President, Bravo remarked to him: "Perhaps we shall enjoy peace during the four months that you are President." And Paredes replied: "I shall not be responsible for that, nor for my being kept in office. But you can indeed be certain that a lot of blood will be shed if they try to get me out and that my downfall will not be comical like that of the others." I am quite convinced of the truth of these statements.

Esnaurrizar is one of the most insolent and bold-faced pilferers of the public treasury ever seen. He knows how to kick a tottering Government at the same time that he is holding the purse open to help the incoming one. That is the way he has kept his job up to the present time. Believing that the situation today was the same as it had been in times past, he compromised with the revolution, caused the kindhearted Señor Herrera to deal harshly with him, and then went to Paredes and told him that if he needed money he would obtain the necessary funds from his friends. Paredes replied: "I do not need any money but I do intend to make it hard for those who are stealing from the public treasury."

Sunday, the 4th

Fearing that an unexpected summons would oblige me to put myself in the embarrassing position of refusing an appointment as a *representative* on the Council, I went to the Sanctuary[9] at an early hour to spend the entire day outside of Mexico City. At this retreat I learned that I was out of danger and that the firing of the cannon the night before had been occasioned by the election of the President. May God preserve me from the other dangers that I still fear!

I am beginning to be won over to the side of the soldier who has assumed control of our destinies by a bold move which he made today. Tornel was refused the post of Minister of War, and it was given to Almonte. The only favor Tornel obtained was one prompted by feeble politeness, a favor which will serve to mitigate the bitterness of his cup of woe. When he was given the bad news about his rejection, it was suggested that he accept the post of Minister of Foreign Affairs but he refused it.

With all the solemnity characteristic of such events, Paredes today took the customary oath of office in the presence of the so-called Council of Representatives in session in the Chamber of Deputies. Tornel, who did not yet know about the misfortune in store for him, replied to Paredes's address in his capacity as President of the Council.

Monday, the 5th

The mail from Durango has brought bad news about the political situation there. The treacherous garrison, under the command of Colonel Don Francisco Padilla, declared its support of Paredes's plan and tried to force the civil authorities to do the same, under the threat of removing them from office. The authorities resisted, and the troops marched out, occupying Nombre de Dios so that they could obtain the revenues and supplies. The citizens have placed themselves in a state of siege, and it appears that the rebels, commanded by Heredia [former governor of the department] were on their way to attack the city, probably with the idea of re-establishing themselves in their previous positions.

This news, which I learned from sources outside the capital, since no one has written to me, has placed me in a most desperate situation. I had not seen, nor had I wished to see, any of the leaders of the recent revolt, because I was afraid that I would become involved in compromising events by assuming obligations toward these individuals. I had been trying to free myself from just such a predicament. Nevertheless, I could not desert my countrymen in their wretched plight despite the fact that they have been singularly unjust and lacking in gratitude, repaying my unselfish

9 Presumably Guadalupe.

service on their behalf with bitter disappointment of my hopes. Still, their predicament demanded that I forget the past. In any event, I could not forget I was a native of Durango.

Encouraged by those stimulating thoughts, I made the stern sacrifice of requesting an interview with Almonte at the risk of being thought of as an office-seeker and a renegade. I explained the situation to him and begged him to lend his help in doing everything possible on behalf of the authorities in Durango. He received me with the greatest kindness and consideration and offered to do all he could. He also requested me to send messages to the citizens of Durango in the special mail due to be sent out that same night. I wrote the messages and about nine o'clock that night I went to his office with my letters, hoping thereby to influence him at the last moment in providing me with the facilities he had proposed. I walked back and forth in the corridor and had to wait until around half-past ten, and I think my success was complete. In my presence he gave the agreement to the chief secretary. I took the liberty to object several times, and finally he told me to go ahead and dictate the part where I anticipated resistance to the plan on the part of the authorities. Almonte had stipulated as a necessary condition for maintaining them in office *that of their declaration of sympathy with the plan.* Since I had previously advised him that in such cases political expediency demanded not the necessity for taking *positive* action, but rather the necessity for recognizing that *such action should not be taken,* the message was changed. The military commander was advised that in the event the civil authorities had already been dismissed, they were to be reinstated immediately in the exercise of their duties, as indicated in an accompanying message, and that these authorities were to be dismissed *only in the event that they offered open resistance, thereby endangering public tranquillity.* If the citizens of Durango do not escape through this wide gateway it will be their own fault, for I myself am amazed at all I was able to accomplish, especially since what I have done will be nothing less than a reaction against the conquerors. Here is a situation which demonstrates beyond the shadow of a doubt the advantage accruing to a defeated political party when it can depend upon some assistance that can serve as a guarantee of its continued existence in the face of the opposition party. If I had become involved in public affairs and had accepted any of the Ministry posts offered me, I could not have obtained more certain guarantees nor have made my cooperation more effective. It is not at all impossible that ingratitude and anger will charge me with wrongdoing in saving them.

I later had a talk with Almonte about the organization of the Cabinet. He expressed regret that Gordoa had shown such obstinate resistance to accepting the post of Minister of Foreign Affairs and said to me: "Don't be surprised if we knock on your door. We need capable men." I had to commit myself to serve the new Government in any post it might wish to place me except that of Minister. "I shall be your willing messenger,"

I said, "and I shall help in any way I can, on condition that I am not given any public position or one of an official nature."

Almonte told me that he was the one who had told Paredes emphatically that he wanted the post of Minister of War so that he could keep Tornel out. His purpose was to avoid any speculation as to the formation of a political party or the likelihood of a restoration of Government jobs. I have reason to believe that in this maneuver there was also an attempt to discredit Tornel.

That clever manipulator of the public funds, Don Francisco Lombardo, on his own authority had occupied the post of First Secretary of the Ministry of the Treasury since December 31. He had previously been discharged as the result of one of those half-just, half-severe orders issued during the weak, amiable administration of President Herrera. This official wanted to dismiss him for his infamous conduct but since he could not summon the courage to do so, he merely required Lombardo to ask for an indefinite leave of absence with full pay. The rascal was thereby able to get along during the entire administration and kept up a pitiless warfare against the Government as editor of the *Amigo del Pueblo*. He took an active part in the recent revolt until he was thrown into jail. But he thought that he would thereby gain the favor of Paredes and get his job back again. On the 31st he took over his former job under the impression that the *occupation* would maintain him in it, but today he was dismissed with not very flattering words. This fellow was so shameless that he made no secret of his thieving. During the times when he was alone in his office he would say he was having a little *summer vacation* and would then appropriate the funds he wanted.

Anecdote

The corruption during the time that Tornel was Minister got to be so great that he confessed to Gordoa that every now and then his fingers would swell up as the result of his *signing warrants*. Baranda told me that on one occasion all those whose names appeared on the long list of the month's salaries in the Ministry of War were paid *through the mere value of the stamped paper on which Tornel had issued his warrants*. After such confusion the understanding is shocked by the thought of how this nation can survive. Many persons have told me that the issuance of each warrant was subject to a tax, depending upon the nature of the warrant, and this money went into the Minister's pocket. Only in this way can one explain his lavish spending and the quick fortune he amassed. It would have profited the nation greatly if it could have recovered the three million pesos, thereby preventing him from pursuing this course of destruction, immorality, and reaction which countless leaders and generals, suddenly put into power, usually pursue.

Tuesday, the 6th

Señor Don Luciano Becerra, Bishop-elect of Chiapas,[10] has been appointed Minister of Justice. The appointment is a wise one in view of its moral, patriotic, and learned aspects. But I am afraid that the post will not be filled satisfactorily because Becerra has a placid disposition that borders upon indolence, and by training is an enemy of innovations. Time and time again he exasperated me when I served with him on the committee discussing constitutional procedure.

Wednesday, the 7th

Today Mexico City witnessed a spectacle which it perhaps cannot recall ever having seen before: a General who took the trouble to review in detail all the various bodies of troops in his division. Paredes did just that, and furthermore, saw to it that all the soldiers received the pay due them from funds that were more than enough to suffice.

Paredes has issued orders that all the troops are to go through daily drill and on specified days he will conduct the maneuvers with large bodies of soldiers. He keeps them on the go continually. An honorable pride in a knowledge of tactics is permeating the ranks of the leaders and officers.

A great phenomenon. Several businessmen went to see the Minister of Finance [Parres] and offered him money. He replied that *he did not need any just at that time* and that perhaps within a month he would have recourse to their pocketbooks. The preceding Government could not get the most miserly sum even when it went out and begged for the money with promises of making great sacrifices.

New coups d'état! The cleverest and most impertinent of the thieves who have been stealing from the public funds has received his punishment. Don Antonio Esnaurrizar, that old fop and libertine who maintains an expensive household with coachmen, carriages and horses, and three concubines thrown in for good measure, had acquired the fine tact of watching the downfall of a government so that he could seize its funds and give it the final kick, thus getting into the good graces of the victorious party, which he would join later on with his hands full of gold, ready to help in the first struggles. At his own expense he had a monument erected in Santa Paula where he planned to deposit S.A.'s foot.[11] He is the same person who in December offered to maintain a certain number of soldiers to help fight against him and support the national movement on the 6th of that month. Nevertheless, honest Herrera discharged him from his Treasury post, but he later got it back. Paredes has ordered his dismissal, thus carrying out the principle of the maxim which he quoted to him on the 2nd. General Paredes has crowned this *coup d'état* with another that is really

10   State in the southeastern section of Mexico.
11   Text reads: ". . . el pie de S[anta] A[nna]." Ramírez is referring to the leg lost by Santa Anna at Veracruz in what might be termed a skirmish with the French in 1839.

heroic and well-advised. He has replaced Esnaurrizar with the former Minister of Finance, Don Pedro Fernández del Castillo, an eminently honorable man, and, as everyone says, one who is well fitted for the post.

Today the names of the candidates for President of the Council came up for consideration. Valencia, Tornel, and Gordoa were the candidates. Paredes appointed *the second candidate*. Valencia's anger has reached its peak, and I would not be surprised if it gets him into trouble because the idea of vengeance has taken complete possession of him. I am convinced that when Paredes made his choice he was influenced by the political situation and the dictates of his own heart. I am quite sure that he intended to appoint Tornel Minister of War because of the latter's ability and loyal service. But Almonte was decidedly opposed to the appointment as a detriment to the incoming administration. Paredes's iron determination yielded, although with much regret and sorrow. Gordoa, who was present at the time, has given me all the details. It must be admitted that this incident redounds to Paredes's credit.

Orders have been issued relieving Arista of his command of the Army of the North. The man has been sullying himself with graft ever since the Texas conflict.

The Government of President Herrera sent large sums of money to the hero of Puebla, the famous General Inclán, for the purpose of defending the city. It turns out that of these sums not one penny was given to the troops. The money disappeared elsewhere. Paredes has ordered an investigation to find out where this money is and has determined to make a resounding stroke of justice in this case. Herrera finally did ask for complete information about the funds he sent the General, and *my friend* tells me that once more Herrera gave another demonstration of his kind-hearted weakness. He did not find out the precise details, perhaps because he wanted to take some of the blame from Inclán, and, too, because he was grateful for the services that the latter had rendered him. The newspapers told of a similar instance in former times. The Collector of Revenue at Toluca[12] was found to be short a large sum. In order to protect, as he said, *the family honor,* Herrera permitted the money to be given him as an allowance and put it down on the books as income accruing to the family some time before. Although this is the kind of integrity characteristic of men in our country who enjoy the reputation of being honest, I am not in sympathy with it, nor do I believe that it entitles a man to be hailed as provident. It indicates the narrowest of margins between virtue and crime. Strict justice, and justice alone, can give a man the right to be called honest.

Paredes is continuing his active persecution of the *lost tribe* during the twenty-four hours that Valencia is in office. The newspapers say that the deficit amounts to 80,000 pesos, and *my friend* has informed me that

12 Capital of the state of Mexico.

Valencia appropriated 14,000 pesos to pay an urgent debt. This circumstance will have resounding echoes throughout the entire country.

Castillo Lanzas has been appointed Minister of Foreign Affairs as a result of Gordoa's stout resistance. Although they say that Lanzas is a person of some education, they also say that he is not cut out for the job and that he will be absolutely incapable of taking care of it.

Review of the Situation

Saturday, the 3rd

The Council of Notables, called into session to elect a President, was composed of the following persons:

For Aguascalientes—Don Vicente Romero, Don Manuel Arteaga

For California—Don Manuel Castañares, Don José M. Castañares

For Chihuahua—Don Ignacio Gutiérrez, Don José M. Irogoyen (former Senator)

For Coahuila—Don José Musquis, Don Matías Royuala

For Durango—Don José M. R. Natera, Don Antonio Gamiochipi

For Guanajuato—Don Lucas Alamán, Don Luis Parres

For Chiapas—Don Ignacio Loperena

For Jalisco—Don Miguel Pacheco

For Mexico—Don Nicolás Bravo, the Archbishop of Mexico (both serving for the first time)

For Michoacán—Don Ignacio Anzorena, Don Juan N. Almonte (both serving for the first time)

For Nuevo León—Don Bernardo Guimbara (in the former Government), Don Francisco Lazo Estrada

For N. Mexico—Don Diego Archuieta, Don Antonio Otero

For Oaxaca—Don Carlos Bustamante (Deputy), Don Manuel Regules

For Puebla—Don Manuel Diez de Bonilla (newly-elected Senator), Don Miguel Barreiro

For San Luis—Don Ignacio Sepúlveda, Don Pablo Gordoa

For Sonora—Don Ramón Morales, Don Enrique Grimaret

For Sinaloa—Don Pedro Verdugo

For Tabasco—Don Manuel Escobar, Don Francisco Rodríguez

For Tamaulipas—Don Pedro Ampudia, Don Ramón Garza y Flores

For Veracruz—Don José M. Tornel, Don Francisco Lerdo de Tejada

For Yucatán—Bishop Don Manuel Pardo, Don Juan Cano

For Zacatecas—Don Luis del Hoyo, Don Luis Gordoa[13]

Don Valentín Gómez Farías was among the three members absent.

Valencia criticized these choices on the score of respectability, saying: "If I had been in the place of Paredes I would have had the appointments made in the most restricted and refined part of the city and I also would have appointed myself." He is totally unaware of his own position, and

13 Most of the men listed here were associated with the conservatives.

no one can enlighten him on it. He fancies that he is the country's leading citizen and that he has a big reputation and an immense influence. The truth of the matter is that the people were alarmed when they found that he had been included in the new order of things and breathed freely again when they learned of his downfall. His general temperament and the scandals that have occurred within his own family have acted to make him distasteful to the people. Also, among many other factors, is the people's recollection of the bombs and grenades he hurled upon Mexico City on the 7th of July, 1840.

Wednesday, the 7th

The collection of various kinds of currency from all over the Republic has disappeared from the office of the Minister of Finance. The collection is valued at 700 pesos, and suspicion points to Lombardo. Some files of documents have also disappeared. *Ecce homo!*

Monday, the 8th

The Assembly of this department[14] had protested against Paredes's plan and consequently discontinued its sessions.

There was not even a Governor, because everyone in turn made excuses. Paredes cut the Gordian Knot by naming General Salas to take control. When by this action the members of the Assembly were apprised of what benefits would be granted, they declared their support of the plan.

The *Memorial histórico* announces that the governorship of the department has been offered to Tornel, and he has replied, with due consideration of events, that he will assume the post *whenever the Assembly of the department proposes him for the job according to legal procedure.* This announcement indicates that Tornel is thinking of attracting attention in order to gain popularity and that the editors of that journal (who also edit the *Siglo XIX*) will never get beyond using trickery. They, better than anyone else, knew all about Tornel's rascality and downright viciousness, and yet they have always praised him, or kept silent about him while they were leaping like tigers on everybody else for the merest suspicion of graft. Not a few times they engaged in slander just so they could enjoy the pleasure of besmirching someone's good name. Why did they make these distinctions? Because Tornel was letting Cumplido[15] have all he wanted and was telling Otero that he was the bright and shining star, not only of Mexico but of the whole Universe. And men like these are the organizers of public opinion! These fellows, who preach morality and virtue! . . .[16]

14 Department of Mexico.
15 Cumplido was one of Mexico's outstanding editors and publishers of liberal books in the nineteenth century.
16 Here Genaro García notes that the narrative comes to an end.

EDITOR'S NOTE

In the period from January to August 8, 1846, which is not covered by Ramírez, war between Mexico and the United States had broken out. Previously, on January 12, 1846, news had arrived in Washington from Slidell that a rejection of his proposals was practically a certainty. As a result orders were sent to General Taylor in Texas to move his troops to the Rio Grande. The Mexican Government recognized the Nueces River as the boundary. On April 4 the Mexican commander, General Arista, was ordered to attack the Americans. On April 25 the first brief encounter took place between the troops of the two nations near Matamoros; hostilities had begun, and the declaration of war took place on May 13. In early May the Mexicans were twice defeated in small battles by Taylor and in June and July the Americans occupied Monterrey and California and began their moves into New Mexico. While these military events were taking place Santa Anna, in Cuba, was negotiating with Polk about the possibility of returning to Mexico. The Government of the United States finally allowed him to do so, apparently in the belief that with the overthrow of Paredes the war might be stopped and matters could be settled by negotiation.

In Mexico the liberal leader, Gómez Farías, was doing his best to try to overthrow the Paredes Government. As part of his plan he negotiated with Santa Anna. The latter convinced him that he had become a federalist and that if he were allowed to return he would establish federalism in Mexico. This was agreed upon and on July 31 the long expected revolt began. Its success was assured when General Salas pronounced in Mexico City; Paredes resigned and Salas became the acting President. That he was closely associated with Gómez Farías was evident from the proclamation that new congressional elections would be held on September 27; freedom of the press was re-established on August 7; on August 22 the Constitution of 1824 was declared to be in effect. In the meantime, on August 16, Santa Anna, with the permission of the American squadron near Veracruz, was allowed to land there.

With the exception of the letter from Santa Anna to Ramírez dated January 19, 1847, all the remaining letters, beginning with that dated August 22, 1846, were written by Ramírez to General Francisco Elorriaga, Governor of the state of Durango.

CHAPTER III

SANTA ANNA ASSUMES POWER

Confidential Memorandum

August 8[1]

What the *Republicano*[2] says about S. A. has been verified. A special message has arrived telling of the agreement between the Commodore of the American squadron and the English Commander not to permit anything but the shipment of quicksilver to be sent ashore. A boat from the harbor where the packet ship is anchored will put out to receive the shipment. I have received this information from a person who always has authentic news. It was also said there was a possibility that S. A. was no longer in Havana when the packet ship arrived there, and that he had gone to Yucatán, in which case he would make the journey by land with perhaps some danger.

The city of Puebla began to cause serious uneasiness, and this morning a division of troops was to have left to keep order there. But at five o'clock this afternoon the city's loyalty was announced amid the firing of cannon and the ringing of bells. Domingo Ibarra is now the Governor, the other authorities not wishing to continue in office.

It is still maintained today that the last division of troops which left the capital for the interior under the command of Don Simeón Ramírez will not recognize the new order, not even with General Paredes in jail. Nevertheless, I cannot bring myself to believe that good comrades will come to blows over such a trifle.

General Paredes's imprisonment does not demonstrate his *obvious* bravery, as is generally thought to be the case among the people here. It was a real misfortune for him, due in great part to his imprudence and his total disregard for taking precautions. Some people have been inferring from this that he was not imprisoned without his consent, but I look upon the whole business as an indication of ill will against him. He saw that he was in exactly the same situation as the criminals of ancient times who were compelled to choose between the dagger and the cup of poison. It appears evident that he made up his mind to link his future with that of the Government, notwithstanding the fact that those in power were openly hostile to him. But while he was loading his pistols to put himself at the head of a column of troops to attack the rebels, he was told that the regiment that formed the body of troops had gone over to the enemy.

Although the Government forces were inferior in number to the attackers, they would have been more than enough to resist them successfully, considering how disorganized and cowardly the latter were. It had

1 In the year 1846. See Editor's Note at the end of preceding chapter.
2 Newspaper in Mexico City. It was anti-Farías.

been announced that the attack on the President's Palace was to begin at three o'clock in the afternoon.[3] When I saw that all was still quiet my curiosity got the better of me, and I went to have a look at the attacking troops, who were drawn up in formation on the Calle de la Acordada. I found the preliminary maneuvers had already begun, but the immense crowd of onlookers was pressing in upon the troops. There was artillery, cavalry and infantry. A host of revenue officials were among them, armed with muskets. These officials called themselves *The Sacred Phalanx*. The rear guard was flanked by *twelve carriages ostensibly reserved for medical corps men*, but filled with curiosity seekers. The whole column began to march, and as it approached the Calle San Francisco its progress was stopped by the surging throng. The commander then ordered the bugle to sound "Enemy sighted!" This was followed by two shots, fired in the air. An astonishing thing then occurred. The echoes had hardly died away when the street became empty except for General Salas and three men of *The Sacred Phalanx*, who had fallen to the ground, thinking that they had been struck by the bullets which had been fired at a distance of seventy yards in front of them. All the others had disappeared. This incident is literally true, just as it is also literally true that fifteen resolute men could have scattered the whole column of troops. Many another scene, still more comical than this one, occurred during those two days. They have filled me with shame because we have been disgraced in the eyes of those who witnessed the proceedings.

I do not understand what is going on. Many of those who were backing this revolution by fighting the Government's unfortunate program are giving indications of being dissatisfied. Among them are two Tapatíos who formulated the plan that has ruined Guadalajara. The spirit prevalent among the other parties can be judged by this turn of events.

Salas is in full charge of the Government, and although Farías is residing in the President's Palace he has no official duties, as the plan itself indicates. The ones who are manifestly the men with authority to govern are Salas, Olaguível,[4] Lafragua and Villamil. When I asked one of these men in what capacity Farías was acting, he replied that he was there as a guarantee and that S. A. had ordered that everything be carried out in agreement with Farías's wishes. He also has issued orders that nothing is to be done until his arrival and even has forbidden the organization of a provisional government. Up until today these orders have been carried out to the letter.

Pedraza has been invited to join his party with that of the winner but he has refused. The same resistance has been encountered in Valencia, who has been living in Tacubaya since the beginning of the quarrel. He

3 August 5.
4 Francisco Modesto de Olaguível, soon to become governor of the state of Mexico.

replied, furthermore, that he would never join forces with anyone friendly toward Farías.

Paredes and his companions in jail are to be held strictly incommunicado until S. A. returns, at which time they will be turned over to him so that he may decide what to do with them. This had been agreed upon from the very first, and although Bravo did all he could to get guarantees from him at the time of the surrender, these guarantees were sternly refused, just as were any guarantees for the party known as the Monarchists. Who knows how much this story will be exaggerated when it comes time to draw up a list of names? You surely ought to know that exile for all suspects was actually considered, and Riva Palacio's name was on the list. There were also a few who had suggested openly that an attack ought to be made on the residence of the Spanish Minister because it had been rumored that Alamán[5] was in hiding there. All these fears have vanished now, and they say that Farías is not so bad a fellow as they feared he might be. Nevertheless, he sent a severe reprimand to Otero, with obvious indications of a threat, and the latter, not knowing what side to take, concluded that he would satirize the revolution which he had once so actively supported.

I say again that I still cannot get a clear idea of the state of things. This situation is likely to turn out to be the most explosive of any we have seen lately, if it does not gain in strength as it develops. The federalists, now in a compromising situation, are doing everything possible to improve their position by trickery. I am very much afraid that their friends plan to give them all the rope possible, demanding proportionate compensation, in order to bring about a repetition of what happened in 1834.[6] What I cannot easily visualize is a directing head capable of carrying out this plan, and this makes me fear that a violent disagreement is going to flare up.[7] Up to today two important measures have been enacted, and an order has been issued today for a levy of troops for the civilian militia. It has not yet appeared in the papers. If S. A. should somehow be eliminated and the other political parties were called upon to cooperate, it would be quite possible for us to save ourselves by a stroke of sheer good fortune. But I can still see that we are in for a period of absolute intolerance, boundless envy, and an eruption of whetted passions. The editor of the *Diario* gave some idea of the situation in yesterday's edition. Our trouble is that we have too many wise men and diplomats who are springing up everywhere.

And what will you do about it? Why, you will say that you are fully aware of the whole business and in no case will you let yourself be bullied.

5 Lucas Alamán was one of Mexico's greatest nineteenth century conservative leaders and, in all probability, one of her greatest historians.

6 This is a reference to the fact that the liberals, under Gómez Farías as acting President for Santa Anna, in 1833-34, had attempted a number of reforms and had been ousted from the Government.

7 It is interesting to note here that Ramírez, like many other Mexicans of the period, apparently could not quite convince himself that the liberals under Gómez Farías and the followers of Santa Anna could work together.

You can easily understand that this letter cannot be shown to anyone—mind you, to anyone—since I should be running a great risk if it were known that I wrote it. If you want to say something about what I have written do not mention my name, and tear this up.

If you wish to show the enclosures to anyone dictate them first so they will appear in someone else's handwriting.

A great many other announcements have appeared on street-corner handbills. The bearer of this letter is not subject to the restrictions I have indicated above.

Mexico City, August 22, 1846[8]

To His Excellency, Sr. D. Francisco Elorriaga

My dear friend:

Between five and six o'clock this afternoon there were published, by a most solemn proclamation amid the din of pealing church bells, the two decrees which you surely ought to receive by the present courier, unless the decrees themselves prevent you from receiving the news. The Constitution of 1824 has been reinstated, in so far as it agrees with the plan promulgated by the men in the *Ciudadela* and with the amendments and restrictions which will later become evident. We must agree that S. A., although strictly a soldier, has more ability than the Monarchists and his very skillful former Minister of War, who boasted to everyone (and I can vouch for it) that he had *revived* the former plan which S. A. had killed and which in my opinion was an undeniable monument to stupidity. My one desire is that this same ability can be shown in carrying out the plan so that we can be saved from the clutches of anarchy and invasion.

General Almonte, who has been universally thought of as S. A.'s advance agent, or at least as a champion of the latter's political theories, reached the capital at the very hour the proclamation was issued. He is considered an advocate of his (Santa Anna's)[9] theories because people believe that he has been commissioned to explore the situation to see what course he (Santa Anna)[10] should pursue. The undertaking is most difficult no matter how simple it looks! The incomprehensible resists any kind of description. I must have a talk with him and really should be at his house now, since I was invited to go out to meet him. But since I am still something of a sinner in S. A.'s estimation and he might suspect that I was trying to put myself forward in order to gain his forgiveness, I refused the invitation on

8   In August and early September, 1846, Taylor made his gradual march into northern Mexico. The new Mexican Government was getting itself organized and waiting for the arrival of Santa Anna, who reached Mexico City on September 14. On August 28 Gómez Farías had been appointed Secretary of the Treasury and began his attempt to obtain the money that had been pledged by the church to the Government for the support of the war. For this section the editor has relied heavily on Hutchinson's *Gómez Farías* for material on internal Mexico.

9   Inserted by translator.

10   Inserted by translator.

the grounds of having a cold. I have intentionally tried to prolong it ever since the day before yesterday just in case any unforeseen situation arose. Since I have had to remain indoors as the result of this decision, I do not have very much news to give you.

I can tell you, however, that two persons of importance have come to see me on a strange mission. Assuming that I had some influence with Almonte, they wanted me to lend my aid in giving the revolution a new turn which would avoid the dangers they fear. This would be done by effecting a union of political parties. Each of my visitors had his own party loyalty, although both expressed themselves in quite moderate terms. But after I had made some effort to analyze the situation, I saw that these men had no plan nor agreement nor anything else and that all those political parties were made up of nothing more than frightful individualists. You might well be amazed, but the most compact and unified is Farías's party, a party which has a wide base but does not reach very high. The reverse is true of the so-called Pedrasista party, which to me looks like an inverted cone.

Are you not overwhelmed at the imprudence (I find myself tempted to call it stupidity) with which this party has conducted itself? It has destroyed, or at least retarded immensely, our whole future. Now that the time has come to sit down to a meal it has broken its fast with putrid meat, which has only done it harm. It had the impertinence to present itself already organized and forming a threatening phalanx in the City Council and the Assembly. It was a challenge to S. A. to put his own men in both governing bodies. It finally crowned its efforts by tricking and knifing the democratic party to which it originally owed its position of influence. Whom could it then rely upon to defend it? What has it accomplished? It succeeded in getting the Commander-in-Chief of the army to start a new political revolution, destroying all governing bodies so that he can get his defeated helpers out of their difficulties. The party has taken advantage of this opportunity to strengthen itself by weakening the position of those who might later give it trouble. In fact, the governors, with the powers afforded them by the old state constitutions, actually have less authority than ever; and if the military chief assumed the right to remove them *ad libitum,* their authority would be reduced to nothing. It is quite strange that since all these gentlemen are professional politicians and do so much boasting that they have superior numbers, they ignore the fact that the fundamental rule of politics is "Bide Your Time."

What do you think of S. A.'s manifesto? I have read it and re-read it and I still cannot understand it. Perhaps I shall learn something profitable in the next mail.

The enclosed letters explain themselves. Please tell my family that I am well.

Mexico City, August 26, 1846

What I have to say is so confused that I shall begin with the first thing that comes to my mind.

As soon as I received your last letter containing the unpleasant news, I went to see Almonte to inform him what was going on in Durango and to beg him to use his influence on your behalf and that of our friends. Our conference was a long and frank one, and from it I gathered that I had made a mistake in the opinion I expressed to you about the decree's restoring the Constitution of '24. General S. A. has made up his mind, at least for the present, to identify himself with the democratic party, appointing Farías, Olaguível and Lafragua his chiefs, much to their delight, and also satisfying Rejón's[11] aspirations. They say Rejón has been completely won over by this gesture. These men have demanded a clean sweep of state governments and assemblies to rid them, as they say, of Monarchists, Decembrists,[12] and Pedrasistas. They are thus completely in accord with the sentiments of S. A., who particularly detests the latter two groups. Of course Almonte did not mention any names nor did he discuss the crux of the difficulty, but he did explain the general idea to me. He added that the dismissals from office were part of this general plan and that it would be difficult to make an exception of you, although he promised me that he would do what he could. Not satisfied with this explanation I went to Lafragua's house to have a talk with him. When I found that he was not at home, I left a message for him in which I asked him to come to see me today. He has not done so, and this has worried me a great deal, because I want you to realize that a certain little point of personal honor had been keeping me from going to see him, although we get along perfectly well. Now he will think that I am trying to have this talk with him because present circumstances are forcing me to do so. I am very much afraid that by the time this letter reaches you, all the fears I expressed to you in my previous communication will have been realized.

Public affairs are becoming truly incomprehensible. There is no doubt whatsoever that S. A. is returning as a real democrat, and I can conceive of his being one, although I cannot tell you on what I base my convictions. Almonte expressed himself to me in the same vein, with ideas that were quite liberal and flattering to all the opinions I had manifested. Of course these opinions on my part were carefully chosen. Baranda arrived last night from Guanajuato[13] and came to see me this morning, telling me that he was amazed at the ultra-liberalism of Rejón, with whom he had had a long conference. Rejón has agreed with all the latest measures and continues to

11　Manuel Crescencio Rejón was an old friend of Gómez Farías and a supporter of federalism. He now was supporting Santa Anna and helped convince Gómez Farías that Santa Anna had changed and that he would now support the liberals.

12　Supporters of Paredes.

13　City in a state of the same name northwest of Mexico City.

direct political activities along with Farías. The stories I have been told about him surpass all fancy and leave me overwhelmed. So that you may judge what my situation is like and try to imagine yourself in my place, I shall tell you that I received three invitations for a conference in which the discussion was to be about ways and means to improve the political scene, and that one of those who had invited me was Rejón. And further: yesterday news got out that I was going to be appointed a member of the future Cabinet. Don Gregorio Mier and Riva Palacio told me personally. I could tell you some more things that would drive you crazy but I shall refrain. What do you make of all these wild happenings?

They have been making a fool out of Morales, although I grant that he has given them plenty of opportunity to do so. They sent him to Guanajuato to resume his civil duties and they did this after they had played with him to their hearts' content. He, the stupid fellow, went on his way, proclaiming that for the present a federation was not the right thing to have. He had not been back at his post two days when the order for his dismissal arrived, and his job was given to a man who Muñoz Ledo says is a ragamuffin. This man is known as a Monarchist. The Querétaro election is the same kind of business because the rule adopted by the men at the *Ciudadela* is that only proved helpers are to be chosen. The capital has been declared a district, and Olaguível has been appointed Governor of the state of Mexico with orders to set up his capital in Toluca. The new organization of the State Supreme Court was announced today, and our poor friend Arriola was not included.

It has been announced that a new decree authorizing a levy of 120,000 national militiamen is to be issued.[14] Although Almonte would not verify the actual number involved, he did confirm my opinion, and in terms so flattering that it would not be discreet to put his reply in writing.

Now let us examine the reverse of the coin.

The troops are giving indications of being quite alarmed, now that the joke seems to be going too far. They have sent their representatives to S. A. to get him to clear up the situation for them; but they have not accomplished anything by that, because the patriots have completely surrounded him and are not letting him out of their sight for one instant. Judging by the various reports I have received, I gather that he is either intimidated or has made up his mind to let matters take what course they may. The officer in command at Veracruz had sent him a detachment of troops to act as his guard, but Baranda assures me that he sent the troops back, saying that he thought he was quite safe among the people. When he was requested to permit an escort of soldiers to accompany him, he asked that this escort be made up of *militiamen from Jico*. These are the troops now with him. You can no doubt imagine the sensation this has caused among the troops,

14 One of the main hopes of the liberals had been to break the power of the army groups. One of the ways in which they hoped to do so was to establish a militia under the control of the civil authorities.

who in fact are beginning to give visible signs of their apprehension. Two or three days ago it was rumored that Valencia was trying to start another uprising for the purpose of proclaiming the permanent dictatorship of S. A. I do not know Valencia's purpose, but the uprising does not strike me as being such a strange idea.

There is still more to this. This morning a special messenger arrived. He was sent by Ampudia, and *the person who saw the messages* tells me they contain information from Ampudia concerning a certain request signed by the officers of the brigade under his command to the effect that Salas should not send them to Texas, and that if they had to go there, then Salas should prevent Paredes from falling victim to S. A.'s vengeance. They furthermore requested that S. A. put Paredes at the head of the army. I had known previously from another source that the messenger had come, but no one had been able to discover what news he carried.

There is conclusive evidence that the unpredictable Miñón has permitted Paredes to stay in the *town* of Perote, at liberty on his word of honor, instead of imprisoning him in the castle as was his duty. Miñón told him that if he made any attempt to run away he (Miñón)[15] would have to commit suicide! If all this is true, I sympathize both with Paredes and with his chivalrous guard, because the news I gave you above makes the former's position a most dangerous one.

I do not believe that any decision has been made up to the present time with regard to the Cabinet, with the exception of Rejón and Almonte. As far as I can determine, they will get posts in it. Farías's post as Minister of Finance seems assured, and there is some talk of Lafragua for Minister of Justice. The latter's appointment does not seem improbable to me because they say it would be as a sort of guarantee. Farías's appointment was delayed until yesterday, since there was a plan to put him on a kind of Council which they intended to organize or to give him a seat in the future Congress so that he might range at will. Nobody knows exactly what will be done.

S. A. is postponing his arrival until the 3rd, and there are some who think that he will postpone it until after that, according to arrangements he is believed to have made. I personally think that he has already made his plans but is not telling even his most intimate associates.

Tornel carried on his fight and came out a beaten man. More than that, he was threatened with reprisals. All parties are united against him. Pedraza has had a slightly less bitter fate, since during the celebrations the democratic element did nothing more than throw stones at his house and link his name with that of Don Lucas Alamán in their cries of "Down

15 Inserted by translator.

with Alamán and Pedraza!" I do not find Urrea identified with any of the political groups.

What opinions have you formed from what I have been telling you? None? Well, that is the way I feel about it all. On the one hand I can find encouraging prospects, but on the other I do not see any elements that will make for stability. Far from it, I actually believe I can see the beginnings of an immense pile of explosives. And who knows whether they will blow us sky-high on the day they are set off? S. A.'s curse levelled against almost all classes and almost all the influential persons in our society, coupled with the shouts of rejoicing with which it was received by his supporters, make me fear that justice does not exist. Nor do I expect much ability in the political organization which is being prepared for us, because as a highly influential individual has expressed it, in such circumstances people do not want *capability* but *men whose loyalty has been proved* and who might be useful for everything except for organizing a country that is falling to pieces, as ours is. Perhaps this would be an opportunity to be seized upon. Still, I say to you with all sincerity that if the present destructive state of affairs gives us the chance to shake off the ominous yoke of the military, I shall agree with everything that comes along. I should do so even if the frenzy of democracy brings us a thousand times greater personal harm than any good we can possibly realize from it, for such a type of oppression is temporary and never irksome. I, for my part, consider only the well-being and honor that can come to my country after the storm has subsided. The situation is extremely difficult, and if we continue to act foolishly it may bring us either a consolidation of despotic military power or the reality of a monarchy that we have been so much afraid of.

As far as you yourself are concerned, I think that if today you do not receive orders to resign, you should continue at your post until you are dismissed, because a resignation might be construed as a hostile attitude toward the present regime and support of the past one. If, however, you are determined to resign, I believe it would be wise to send your resignation in a letter to Almonte and have me deliver it to him; tell Almonte in the letter that I shall inform him of your plans. In this way it will be possible to avoid certain difficulties, for I cannot reconcile myself to the thought of your resignation.

In any event, we must keep on our toes and take advantage of time to work for the coming elections, especially with regard to the internal organization of the department, since we are all in this together. But I hope to heaven that the election does not turn out to be a malodorous affair, because if it does we are in for a devil of a time. Think all this over very carefully and work hard, meanwhile keeping in mind the fact that we are going to work out our plan for salvation in case there is a shipwreck.

Be very careful about how you handle the news I am sending you and also be careful about revealing the identity of the sender.

Mexico City, September 16, 1846[16]

Sr. Don Francisco Elorriaga

My dear friend:

I let several mail collections go by without sending you a letter, because the horizon was decidedly cloudy and I did not wish to waste your time with silly predictions. Today I can see a ray of light, whether of salvation or not I do not know. But at any rate there is something in the wind that indicates a turn of events which might possibly lead to a denouement of some sort. This will be either good or bad according to the elements that contribute to its development.

The preliminary signs are not very consoling. The victorious federalists have determined upon their course of action and have assumed direction of the most hysterical types of transactions. These affairs are the ones given prominent places in the ridiculous pantomimes which the *Republicano* calls *Federalist Society*.[17] They are no more than a farce and a parody of the *meetings*[18] held by the English and the people of the United States. Although the resolutions agreed upon at these assemblies will give you some idea of their nature (you no doubt have read them in the newspapers), it is nevertheless impossible to imagine what kinds of subjects have been discussed in the speechmaking, for you must realize that anyone at all has the right to get up and express his opinions. Indeed, I must tell you that among other matters discussed and given utmost attention were these: First, behead Don Lucas Alamán and all those suspected of being Monarchists, even if it meant an expenditure of 200,000 pesos, as the orator declared, adding that 400,000 pesos had been spent to cut off the head of an illustrious man.[19] It was also suggested that they could arm themselves with daggers and have a regular Sicilian Vespers massacre. The speaker here drew a dagger to emphasize his remarks. The second was to take over church properties and to abolish church privileges. On this subject all kinds of opinions that seemed at all relevant were expressed. The third point covered the closing of the houses for novices, the reason being the alleged corruption and prostitution of the monks who, it was said, maintained mistresses. This was also an occasion for a fierce jab at the secular clergy. Point number four urged the establishment of civil

16 From September 16 to November 7 Taylor continued his march into northern Mexico, and Santa Anna began to organize his army for the coming fight with Taylor. In late September Gómez Farías resigned his Cabinet post to become a member of the new Council which had been established. Elections were held on September 27 for Congress, and Salas was continued as interim President.

17 Behind practically any political movement in the nineteenth century was a "club" or a "society."

18 In English in the text.

19 Footnote in text states: "That of General Don Vicente Guerrero." The reference here is to the scandalous manner in which Guerrero was killed in 1831. Alamán was generally accused of having had a part in the action taken by the Government against Guerrero.

marriages, leaving it to the wish or the conscience of each of the contracting parties whether or not the blessing of the church was to be included. The fifth point referred to the exclusion of Monarchist priests from provincial councils. The sixth dealt with intolerance; the seventh, with limiting the church's general powers and, if necessary, the suppression of the confession. It was alleged that on the pretext of getting confessions the priests reveal family secrets, to the detriment of fathers, husbands, etc. The eighth point incorporated a plan for excluding from public office all men who had reached a certain age: for example, the age of forty, at which age it was suggested public servants were to be dismissed. The fifth point was voted down. The sixth scandalized some of the members with its politico-religious aspects and they even went so far as to interrupt the speaker. The seventh point aroused the ire of a gentleman of the cloth to such a pitch that he shouted, "Down with the heretic!" All the suggestions were applauded more or less, especially the remarks against the army when it was recommended that the national guard be given greater recognition.

Although there is still a great deal that I have not discussed here, this brief summary of what I can recall will give you some idea of the social conditions in which this party has come to play a prominent role, a party determined to make a clean sweep of everything, thereby putting itself in a most exaggerated position. To cap the climax I shall tell you that there was a serious discussion about honoring S. A. with a general plundering of the city and if the situation got serious five Monarchists, at least, were to be hanged from the balconies of their homes. It became necessary to take some determined steps to prevent all this from happening, and the most effective measure was the threat that S. A. would not enter Mexico City. I got this information from the very man who worked hard to keep these things from taking place.

I am convinced that the news of these and many other developments which would require too much time to discuss induced S. A. to make up his mind not to enter the capital. His decision placed the Government in a most embarrassing position. The ministers have nothing in common and distrust one another. For this reason no one could even go to El Encero[20] to resolve the difficulty because those who remained behind mistrusted the one who left, while the latter was fearful of what the others would do in his absence. This is the conclusion I have arrived at from an analysis of the situation, a conclusion confirmed by the compromise they reached. It was finally decided to send Baranda as a representative or emissary of the Government to exact three promises from him (Santa Anna):[21] One, that he would enter Mexico City; two, that he would immediately assume control of the Government; and three, that he would not establish his residence in Tacubaya. You probably have seen the decree issued for the

20 One of Santa Anna's haciendas east of Mexico City.
21 *Santa Anna* was inserted by translator.

purpose of compromising him still further by announcing that S. A. will assume the Presidency on the day he arrives, etc., etc. But they were careful to conceal all this from Baranda, since the decree was issued after he left and sent on to him in charge of a prominent person who delivered it in Ayotla.[22] Farías especially urged Baranda to tell S. A. that it would be considered an open act of hostility toward the people if he did not come into the city, and the other ministers expressed the same opinion. S. A. decided to acquiesce to the demand, and his reply to the other two points[23] is contained in his message which the press has eulogized so much, for which it was well paid.

Farías headed the delegation that went out to Peñón[24] to receive S. A. There was a heated argument to get him to change his plans, but he maintained a firm attitude and even remarked that he would not even dine in Mexico City. This turned out to be quite true. The banquet that had been prepared for eighty[25] guests was called off. But let us get back to the business about his entry into the city. Disregarding all the farcical stuff in the newspapers, I shall tell you that the whole affair was a decidedly democratic one: not a frock coat nor a carriage other than those of the officials. S. A. rode in the Government's state coach, an open carriage. He sat there on the main seat, sunk down among the cushions, with the big banner of the federal constitution fluttering from its staff at his right. The size of the banner with its attached streamers and tricolored ribbons made it almost impossible for him to sit down. Farías rode on the front seat, facing him and the banner. Both men were silent and seemed more like victims than conquerors. S. A. was dressed in quite a democratic fashion: a long traveling coat, white trousers and no crosses or medals on his breast. So terrible was the impression all this produced on me that when the coach got to a place opposite my balcony windows, I drew back involuntarily, being seized with such a violent headache that I was no good the rest of the day. I do not know what sort of terrible, foreboding thing I could possibly have observed in that scene.

When he (Santa Anna)[26] got to the Palace the people surged in everywhere from the Crimson Room to the President's private bedroom, and even at five o'clock in the afternoon (he had entered the Palace at two), I could still see on the balconies of the Crimson Room a great many in high-crowned hats and side-button trousers who were watching the troops march by and witnessing all the other celebrations in the plaza. A short time later he (Santa Anna)[27] left for Tacubaya after requesting eight or ten *intimate* friends to accompany him there for dinner. After the list of these friends

22 Small town east of Mexico City.
23 He refused to comply with the Cabinet's last two requests.
24 Small town east of Mexico City.
25 The text states *ocho* (eight) but probably the correct figure in *ochenta* (eighty) as stated in Riva Palacio, *Mexico a través de los siglos*, IV, 578.
26 Inserted by translator.
27 Inserted by translator.

was drawn up, Rejón added Bas, the speaker at the first *meeting*, the famous Carvajal Don Vicente Romero and his son, Eligio, who is even more important than the father. Rejón stated that S. A. ought to be in the company of the leading men among the people, etc., etc. The evening was spent in merrymaking, and Bas, who had eaten and drunk more than was good for him, refused some pastries on the excuse that he could eat them only if they were seasoned with a certain kind of meat. His idea was to cut off some heads, although he did not say this openly to S. A.

He (Santa Anna)[28] is telling everyone he sees that he does not intend to remain in Mexico City any longer than absolutely necessary for him to obtain funds, and he has set his time limit at a week. He says that he is not going to leave a single soldier within the city but will concentrate the whole army in San Luis, even if the corps are reduced only to their officers. He will fill out the corps until he has assembled 25,000 effective troops. He has demanded an assurance of 300,000 pesos a month to maintain them. This is to be done not in a haphazard fashion but by contract, in which the person assuming the obligation will pay him the money directly without the Government's having any part in the transaction whatsoever.

The big difficulty that came up involved the choice of a successor. Salas did not want to continue in office, either because of illness or anger, since he did not think he had any right to act in an executive capacity when S. A. had appeared on the scene. The latter's refusal to take responsibility, coupled with the reasons he gave for this refusal, has made the illegality of the situation all the more evident, and yet even up to this morning it looked as if he (Santa Anna)[29] were still determined to maintain the present state of affairs. In spite of all this, however, I fancy that there will soon be quite a striking change in the make-up of the Cabinet, although I cannot even guess how far this will go. But there will be repercussions.

I cannot say much more, nor do I think that what I could say would be essential to enable anyone to get a more or less accurate idea about what may happen. You will undoubtedly observe that it still can be said today that events are so progressing that it is possible to make them take the direction one wishes. But I doubt that this possibility will last much longer, considering the lengths to which our liberals will go the moment they think that all restraints are off. They will conclude that they are entitled to do anything that comes to their minds; and worst of all they will be firmly convinced that any such course of action will have to be maintained. Today, as was to be expected, they are making every effort to assure the victory of their partisans in the coming elections. Although the establishment of the capital as a separate district deprives them of their great support, they are sparing no effort to compensate for this loss by whipping

28 Inserted by translator.
29 Inserted by translator.

up the same reactionary spirit in the departments. I really cannot entertain any hopes for the good judgment of my compatriots; and although
considering the state of affairs as they are today I am frankly and loyally
in favor of federation, I believe that the men who finally established it
have such wild plans that they could even terrify the republicans in the
United States to the point of rising in revolt. Some of the things I have
heard these men say fill me with fear, because I cannot find in their remarks
even a grain of common sense. It seems to me that the total dismemberment and independence of the departments would be a thousand times
preferable. It is easy to see what all this may bring down upon our heads,
and in order that you may not think my refusal of your two invitations
was a result of any foolish whim on my part, I shall tell you that I am not
inclined to accept a post as representative from Durango. We have reached
a point where it is impossible to keep a middle course. Either the total
destruction of the Republic or its preservation will be decided in the next
Congress, if it ever convenes.

I have it on the *best* authority that S. A. wanted to have a talk with
Pedraza to see what could be done about a union of the two parties and
that upon receiving the request the latter meekly consented to come
to the conference. S. A. had formulated a plan to bring Pedraza and
Farías together. No one knows at this time whether the beginnings of the
merger are under way, since several days ago Pedraza went to Tacubaya
to live because he was afraid to remain in Mexico City. I do not think it
impossible that the former will soon achieve his objective, even though he
stirs up quite a lot of opposition. I also consider it very probable that
there will result from his plan more and more festering schisms which, in
short, he can use to his own advantage, since it is the means of overcoming
other difficulties.

I did not want to take any part whatsoever in these developments
and have kept my relations with Almonte and Rejón cool and formal.
This is going to make it more difficult for me to confront a new situation
that is threatening me or, rather, one that I am having to deal with right
now. It is a situation which by its very nature is like the sharp point of
a needle. Paredes has been foolish enough to send a memorandum to the
Government requesting that he either be provided with a passport to enable
him to leave the Republic or be granted the privilege of being tried before
judges appointed by the Government. He has invoked the guarantees of
the federal constitution for this purpose. After he took this step he informed his family, and they have asked me to act as his attorney! What
do you think of that? Knowing me as you do, you no doubt will have
already guessed what my answer will be.[30] This happened today and has
upset me so much that I do not know which way to turn. I shall have to
cultivate friendships which I have been trying so carefully to avoid. How

30 Ramírez accepted and on September 18 was able to obtain a passport for
Paredes.

much I need S. A.'s friendship right now! Deep down in my heart I feel that I could derive great advantage from it. Keep the account of this incident to yourself; I have told you about it to ease my mind.

It is time to mail this, and I have written too much. Goodbye.

Please forgive the expense and annoyance that I am causing you by making you responsible for forwarding the enclosed messages.

Mexico City, September 23, 1846

My dear friend:

I shall begin by placing at your disposal my privileges as a federalist, which I secured without resorting to the vice of either secrecy or fraudulence, so that I am perfectly free to speak my mind or keep silent as I wish. You understand that I am talking about the position of Council member, which finally fell to my lot together with another painful obligation that will also be my share. Let us get on to something else. I want you to listen to a curious story that fairly chilled me when I heard it, because I can plainly see that we are in the power of an influence which . . . but who can say? Let us get to the point.

It was decided that Farías was an obstacle to the onward march of the Government and the political bosses, and S. A. without consulting anyone simply sent a memorandum to Rejón containing the list of names of Council members. He added, as if it were a mere afterthought, that since the post of Finance Minister would be made vacant by the promotion of Farías to the presidency of the Council, that post could be filled by Haro,[31] whom he ordered to be summoned by special messenger. A bomb could not have produced greater amazement than this order. Rejón flew into a rage, and even Farías was extremely upset. They said that if it were an open break that was wanted, there would certainly be one, and they called S. A. an ingrate and other things besides. They ended their remarks with the statement that the Cabinet would resign *in a body*.

Baranda was present at the time and, although it was night, he secretly left and went to Tacubaya to tell him what was going on, painting the entire scene with colorful words of apprehension and profound worry. S. A. listened to him very calmly and told him that it was not his intention to quarrel with Farías, much less to displease him. The offer concerning the post of Minister of Finance would be valid *only if there were a vacancy*. He added that, by the same token, if Farías would not accept the presidency of the Council the other offer would be withdrawn, and matters could go on as they had before. He then stated, still as calmly as ever, that Pedraza would be made president of the Council, because it was his intention that the president of that body should substitute in the absence of the President of the Republic, a situation that was likely to arise in view of

---

31 Antonio Haro y Tamáriz was a conservative.

the fact of Salas's ill health. That was why he wanted to have a reliable man for the job.

Baranda left with this news, and as he was going back to Mexico City he met the ministers, who were on their way to Tacubaya. He told them about his (Santa Anna's)[32] decision, and Rejón was more horrified with the idea than he had been previously, because he could see that the affair was taking on an entirely different aspect. But the ministers went on to Tacubaya from where they returned that night faced with the task of making Farías accept the post which was distasteful to him. The ministers went to Farías's home, and since they were accompanied by an escort of soldiers Farías got the idea that they were coming to arrest him and take him out of the city. They could not get him to open the door. Finally, after an exchange of questions and answers, he admitted the ministers. Rejón explained to Farías the facts of the situation. Everything was then settled, and Farías, recovered from his fright and now quite apologetic, said that he was ashamed of what he had said and done and added that he would accept the presidency of the Council. That is the story in a few words, and you may get any kind of moral from it that you see fit. Farías is no longer Minister of Finance, and tomorrow they will probably swear in Haro, who had expressed his unwillingness to accept. The *puristas*[33] are unhappy over the whole affair and are making threats. I believe that Farías is now beginning to realize his position and that of his associates. That leaves only Rejón and he keeps on with his highflown ideas about everything. He is determined to maintain the *federalist meetings*. Recently in these *meetings* they have been discussing the feasibility of permitting priests to marry. There have also been discussions of similar foolish matters.

The clergy have agreed to lend a large part of their country property to back a loan soon to be made. The assistance which the clergy has given constitutes the principal funds which have been used to fight the war. S. A. is to leave the day after tomorrow, and there will be *not one* soldier left in the city.

Be careful how you repeat the story I have told you about Farías even though our friend Señor Castañeda does not figure in it at all, because you no doubt realize that people might exaggerate it.

You have more than enough reason to believe that you have brought your political mission to a worthy, decent end. This is not only the opinion of your friend, who himself could admit making mistakes, but of many other persons who have talked with me and whose word can be relied upon, whether they be Greeks or Trojans. Poor Morales has not been able to get out of it so gracefully. He did a great many foolish things and in his talk with me today expressed his deep regret.

32 Inserted by translator.
33 The *puros* were the more extreme wing of the liberal party.

On the other hand, I say that you will be very foolish and will cause me great regret, which you can understand, if you refuse a job which I have been told they have offered you. It is a job that can provide you with security in your OLD AGE. There, I write it in capital letters so that you will realize that it pertains to you more than you might care to have it. I do not know what kind of a job it is, but I presume that it is one worthy of your social position and proportionate to your virtues; for example, causing me to be exiled from Durango in the glorious year 1826.

Farewell.

I am going to ask you to tell me *frankly* what they are saying there about my position on the Council, especially the *unfavorable* things, because I think it ought to amuse me.

Mexico City, September 26, 1846

My dear friend:

The hopes which I confided in you in my previous letter have vanished, and my fears have been realized. At the very moment I was writing to you everyone was expecting a political reaction which, unless God did not perform a great miracle, could stop all our quarreling, even putting an end to our national life.

Farías resented the blow he had received, and Wednesday night there was a meeting of the *mitineros*, or *mitoteros*,[34] as they are called here. They deliberated on the fundamental decree of the Council and declared it contrary to the law and anti-national, giving as their reasons that it was outside the limits of the constitution, that it was superfluous, etc., and above all that it was prejudicial to the interests of *those who aspire to become deputies*. It was agreed to make a representation against it, and a list of the members' names was drawn up so that the action would be construed as representing the opinion of the entire country. It was also declared that since Salas was holding his Government post illegally, he ought to be dismissed and the post given to Farías, who had national sentiment, legally represented by the *mitineros*, on his side.

You will immediately get the idea that all this uproar was brought on by a feeling of hostility toward the Pedrasistas, or Decembristas, who were cleverly flattered by an offer of complete control in the coming election. This wretched party or, rather, its constituents, who join their ambitions with their foolish policies and their cowardice, got frightened at the storm. Going back on their honorable commitments and their obvious duties, they fled at the first signs of danger, and those who had been named to the Council hurriedly resigned. Pedraza, the first one to pledge himself, since he had made his own *personal* commitment to S. A., was the first to break ranks, and his associates joined him. His behavior has made

34 *Mitineros* from *mitin* (meeting)—i.e., those given to attending meetings; *mitoteros*—jolly fellows.

me angry, not so much because it affects me personally, but because of the frightful future it prepares for us. These men did not think about that. Or perhaps they were incapable of foreseeing such a development. I want you to know that I accepted that accursed position[35] on Almonte's assurance that all the members had pledged their word and that not one would resign.

But putting all this aside and getting back to the gist of the matter, I ask you what hope is there for order; what guarantee can the Government count on in the future, not to mention the national Congress? They are under the rod of a handful of demagogues to whom they have accorded the right to resist their edicts. What sort of hope is there for those sections of the country that have been honored by the title of Sovereign States? How about their representatives, if all of them must submit to the caprice of a political faction? I feel terrified when I think about the future. Now that those gentlemen, concerned only with their own fears and selfish interests, have put the capstone to our misfortunes by refusing to help the Government, which they ought to uphold in this crisis, I will have no hand in the business. Come what may, I shall continue along the path that my blind Destiny is preparing for me. If the Government retreats, it will not be my fault. If it does as it ought and fills the vacant posts without giving quarter to its silly little enemies I shall resign, because I only wish to be a part of it in misfortune and peril. I had a talk last night with Almonte and mentioned my determination to resign; but now that the philosophers have caused my name to appear in print in today's *Republicano* in connection with assigning me to *Don Simplicio's*[36] jurisdiction, I have not tendered my resignation.

Since in our unfortunate country everything is done for persons and nothing for principles, the Council is going to be shipwrecked on this maze of petty passions. In my opinion, the Council is one of the most vital elements in our social order, especially under such scatterbrained systems as ours, where men appear on the political scene and then disappear, like the fleeting figures thrown on the screen by the magic lantern. And what men they are! Usually they are ignorant. You have been an administrator and you have acted in good faith. How often must you have wished for a responsible Council! Several days ago I intended to publish a pamphlet that would give some information about this institution that has been proscribed by the destructive, democratic fury. I was prompted to do this because of the mass of nonsense appearing in the *Republicano*. But I was afraid that people might think that I sympathized with the Monarchists and that my emotions were speaking louder than my convictions, and I

35 Ramírez is referring to his membership on the new Council presided over by Gómez Farías. Also on the Council were the following: Manuel Gómez Pedraza, Juan Rodríguez Puebla, Manuel Baranda, Ignacio Trigueros, Luis de la Rosa, Francisco María Lombardo, Bishop Manuel Pardío, General Martín Carrera Mariano Otero, José María Lafragua and Bernardo Guimbarda. Practically every political ideology is herein represented.

36 *Don Simplicio* was a liberal Mexican journal.

therefore kept quiet because I was afraid of being slandered just as today I am keeping quiet because of propriety. If God grants me the privilege of ever getting out of this slime, I shall speak up. And if you and my associate Castañeda express your approval of the institution (but not out of deference to me) such an expression might lend more weight to my opinions, influenced as they are by consideration for the Government. It would help me form a mature judgment in order to support this point of view in the next reform of the constitution. When we were in the Senate there were always those who would have liked to get rid of the Council, being prompted more by hostility than by principle. That is why I wanted to find out what you think if it. One of the documents I saw was a record book in which I discovered that during the Council's two brief years of existence *one thousand seven hundred-odd* transactions had been up for discussion, and that of these *some eight hundred* had been carried through successfully. That was enough to give me a basis for my opinion, for I cannot even conceive of our ministers' being able to decide definitely upon so many pieces of business in view of the way our cabinets are organized. The only fault that I found in the Council was its organization, because the members did not work as much as they should have. But let us bury this subject. I was beginning to forget that I was writing a private letter.

We are on the eve of an election storm. I do not suppose that it will be either severe or doubtful as to its outcome, because the so-called *moderado* party[37] is eminently helpless. I sent you three of the current lists of candidates. I do not have the other two. The twin lists are well organized into one, and the candidates will win. The other lists of candidates are those of the opposition party, which is not showing a tendency to act in unison even under these circumstances. Tomorrow I shall vote—with four lists! I am trembling at what may happen, for I fear the spirit of of giddiness is everywhere. Now more than ever before we need prudence and wisdom, because if any seed of disunion is sown now it will bear fruit later on and strangle us. We must make mutual sacrifices to maintain harmony. I presume that in Durango certain sympathies, so long suppressed, will be aroused, and I am afraid that they will engulf our friend Castañeda if he insists on backing certain individuals. Talk to him like a friend and like a good citizen of Durango and keep him from dashing himself to pieces on the rock of public opinion. In this way you could accomplish something without risking everything. Although I am far from considering myself a person of sufficient influence to be able to tip the scales one way or the other, I nevertheless have avoided subjecting myself to the test. For this reason, among others, I have decided to postpone my return, because I do not want to be there at a time of election strife. When this is over you can again count on me.

Rumor has it here that you were appointed inspector of the city

37 The *moderados* tended more toward the center than did the *puros*.

militia *at a salary of 4,000 pesos.* I have given the lie to this statement and have done so rather sharply, because the whole thing looked like gossip to me.

Show this to Señor Castañeda. I mean, read to him those parts which do not concern him. Don't either of you fall asleep. Speak clearly, forcefully and logically, so that everyone will understand that the states not only want to rid themselves of the yoke of militarism and oligarchy, but the yoke whatever it may be. Tell the people that a handful of impudent ragamuffins have no right to usurp the good name of the Nation, not even for the purpose of subjugating it by their use of that name.

In spite of the heavy downpour I am going to interrupt my letter and get on to the Palace so that I can send you more fresh news, if there is any.

I returned at nine o'clock tonight without anything's happening which pleased me.

Almonte has such an impassive expression on his face that one cannot tell whether he is giving advice or is speaking *ex abundantia cordis.*[38] He tells me that S. A. sent for Rejón today to get him to ask Pedraza for an explanation and to remind him of his promises, with the further statement that he (Santa Anna)[39] still cannot bring himself to believe that Pedraza wants to go back on his word. I doubt all this because Otero, in speaking about Pedraza, Rosa, and himself, assured me that Pedraza would keep his promise. However, since these three men have been dismissed by their boss, they may easily switch their party allegiance. Almonte also informed me that they were going to proclaim an explanatory decree on the congressional elections in order to remove the doubt or embarrassment that is bothering some consciences.

Be careful how you quote my letters, because otherwise those persons who are no particular friends of mine will see that what I have said gets back to the capital.

(Signature)

What do you think of the article in the *Diario?*[40] The insult handed to us has reached its peak. CONFIDENTIAL—The ministers of the foreign powers have had a conference with Government officials. They asked that permission be granted their subjects to bear arms in defense of their interests *and that a definite place be assigned to these persons for use as a barracks.* Copies of the paper were bought up and will be shipped out on the next packet boat. I wonder what the pretext for intervention will become now? Zerecero is the editor who wrote the article. Unfortunately, Rejón protects all those who deal in exaggerations and is the most enthusiastic of the *mitineros.* Of course he is; it (the meeting)[41] was his invention.

38 From the fullness of his heart.
39 Inserted by translator.
40 The article was published on September 23 and produced much alarm. It reported that the enemy was moving on Monterrey and urged the nation to rise in a body to support the Government.
41 Inserted by translator.

Mexico City, November 7, 1846[42]

My dear friend:

I can see by your letters that you are despondent, and my silence indicates that I consider your state of mind a sad one. You are right about everything, and yet I do not deserve to be even a part of the reason for your annoyance. The events that have transpired here were so complicated and of such unusual and strange character, that to tell you the truth I did not know what to say; I was afraid that I might mislead both of you, as I apparently have. Many days have passed, many secrets have come to light and many mistakes have been rectified; still these events cannot be explained in the customary way. One thing is certain, and that is that the city might have found itself plunged into all kinds of horrors, and our poor reputation might have been sullied with shameful crimes without any plan that could be called political. The hatred that divides the two parties branded as the criminals, and the passions that have flared up between them are the only key to the puzzle. Your letter has given me more light on the situation than all that I could have found out here. I see clearly that the *puros* convinced S. A. that Salas was intending to fling himself into the arms of the enemies whom he fears and hates most. There were plenty of outward indications of this, because three of your friends induced Salas *on the spur of the moment* to shut himself up in the *Ciudadela* along with all the rest.[43] I have been able to see things from a distance and objectively, and I think that all of them were right. The *puros* were right because the first decision was to seize Rejón and Farías and immediately ship them out of the country. The *moderados* were right, because they had good reason to believe that the *puros* were trying to incite an uprising that could cost them their heads. The disinterested parties and finally the citizens as a whole were right, because there was talk of sacking the city, an occurrence not at all improbable once the lower classes were given free rein. The intentions of the politicians in all this were as despicable as their methods of action. Each group sought to get the better of the other so as to assure itself of success in the elections and consolidate its power thereby. I once confided in you my suspicions that a certain person was exaggerating things in order to pave the way for absolute authority for S. A.

42   From November 7 to December 23 the northern Mexican cities of Tampico and Saltillo were occupied by the Americans. On November 18 General Scott was appointed to command the American expedition against Veracruz. In Mexico the battle between the *puros* and *moderados* continued to rage, with the *puros* gradually getting the better of it.

43   Both the *moderados* and *puros* had their own militia, and civil war had almost broken out on October 18. Salas had retired to the *Ciudadela* and had ordered the arrest of Rejón and Gómez Farías, but their forces obtained control of the Palace. Trouble was averted and at least a temporary agreement was reached.

But today I am beginning to have my doubts. S. A. wrote to this person, bluntly approving the latter's removal from office. The letter in reply was couched in violent words, and the relations between the two men became exceedingly strained. On the other hand, it is clear to me that S. A.'s intelligent followers, who are his real support, are not backing Rejón, whom they despise. Farías has adopted another line of incomprehensible conduct. He has been *in hiding* ever since the day of the quarrel and has not permitted even his intimate friends to see him.

This brief summary of events will convince you that the federalist party is finding itself in a most fearful state of anarchy. This is not due simply to its principles but rather to its wretched passions, a development that is not new, since this kind of behavior has always produced the same effect. Where are the federalists going to lead us? It is hard to foresee. As Quintana Roo says, the elections[44] are *a mixture of good and evil*. I cannot be sure that he is speaking the truth, because I am not acquainted with most of the persons concerned. But it is true that with few exceptions, such as in the case of the Veracruz contests, they are all of the same political faith, with here and there a few superficial differences. No one knows the hue they will eventually take on. Everyone agrees that, from what they can see now, Rejón's banner will go on waving without opposition in the Congress. It is impossible to distinguish among the known members of Congress or those newly elected ones who could come forward and take the victory from Rejón. You may say what you will, but Rejón is a man of talent and spirit. These two qualities coupled with a great amount of daring produced by his hatred for his opponents and encouraged by the sizable number of votes that he already has, make him a power worthy of being feared. Add Farías's talents and those of other persons you know, and you can judge what the rest will be.

I have mentioned Farías because I have been assured that his party in Guadalajara has the advantage over the moderate Pedraza party. The latter selected Otero for its candidate when it saw that here and in the state of Mexico it had lost the election. But they also say that another group of moderates is offering opposition, and it is supposed that these will lose out in the contest just as Pedraza lost out in the Querétaro election. We shall find out all about this the day after tomorrow. Even if the election goes in favor of the Pedraza group I cannot see how Otero can keep up his fight against Rejón. Rejón will drag out the struggle over the entire field in which the party is working and in which Otero is notably weak. Rejón is bound to give a scholarly character to the discussion and thereby will succeed at best in getting the Congress to split into separate groups which can do nothing useful. As far as other matters are concerned I do not think it at all impossible that after a few days of fumbling and chaotic activity,

44 The elections of late September. The Congress chosen at that time would later in the year elect the President and Vice-president.

the Congress may settle down to a definite program, because its disorganized character is a favorable element for fusion, if there is someone around who can adopt a course that all can understand. If the whims of Congress will not be satisfied, at least its faith will not be offended. The gamble is going to be over the life or death of the nation, and if I cannot now see that such a development is possible, and I have made mistakes in judgment before, at least let us agree that there is a possibility of a repetition. We are going to put up our last peso after sacrificing all we once had.

The deputies are beginning to arrive, and I understand that all of them are supposed to be in a hurry to perform their duties. Formerly they feared for their safety and their liberty. Up to now it does not seem that they are running any personal risks. All they have to do is to fight against their irrational feelings and they will clearly see what is actually needed for the best interests of the country. They must act accordingly even if it costs them some sacrifices. The most odious matter and one that has been the very source of all our misfortunes was dispensed with today, because I do not suppose that anyone will question the form of Government. For good or ill we must carry on with it as it is, only purging it of its imperfections and adapting it to the conditions of our country. I presume that you, as my good friend, have seen to it that I shall not have to get mixed up in those quarrels. By the same token I urge you to see that our deputies[45] get here quickly, for there is danger in delay. The question of peace or war depends upon the Congress, for already there have been proposals to make peace. It is urgent that funds be raised at once to continue it. In short, the nation must be organized. It has never before been in a greater state of confusion.

I cannot fully express to you the bitterness and indignation which have been aroused in me by the news you sent me concerning the most recent invasion by the barbarians.[46] I do not suppose that I have ever felt so overwhelmed, perhaps because I could not find any means to anticipate or observe this evil occurrence. Our friend Castañeda has sent me no word in the recent mails. I really cannot understand how you and he ever got the idea that the humble influence of a friend could cure all the ills that are afflicting you if he does not know what remedy to ask for. I found myself in precisely this predicament when I went to have a conference with the ministers. I found them sympathetic and was received cordially but nevertheless I left without accomplishing anything, and was quite embarrassed besides. "What do you want done?" they asked me. And I could not even give them an answer, because I had not been instructed what to ask for. I have been bringing this lack of cooperation to your attention ever since you first took up your Government duties, pointing out to you the difference between *asking a favor in the name of friendship* and demanding

45 The deputies from Durango.
46 The nineteenth century Mexican continually used the term "barbarian" when he spoke of Indian invasions of the northern states.

the approval of some measure your Government may see fit to propose. In my opinion complaints should not be voiced unless they are accompanied by a definite proposal to correct the abuses. This has not been done, but something has been done which has brought about the results I foresaw. The official newspaper in your state has never shown discretion in its eulogies; by its praises it gives encouragement to people whom it should never have encouraged, knowing their records, and it exaggerates the nature of even the meanest types of service. It relegates to oblivion those who serve it or who might be in a position to be of help. In this way it finds that it has been caught in the meshes of its own net when some situation arises demanding censure. Indeed, it would seem that it is forbidden to criticize evil deeds. There can be no doubt that most of our ills come from the ineptitude of the leader whom, nevertheless, the *Registro* has overwhelmed with undeserved praise, thereby causing a good opinion of him to be held by the people here. Shall I ask for an interview with no data to depend upon, with no set purpose in mind and without the support of your Government to report that everything is going badly in that part of the country? I have been obliged to do just this time after time and as a result I have obtained only temporary benefits. I cannot reconcile this lack of moral energy, this fear that you gentlemen have always shown on such occasions, because this involves you as well as Castañeda—I repeat: I cannot reconcile these things with other things you have done wherein more courage was necessary, but which nevertheless were carried out successfully. It is obvious, however, that the fear of offending this person or the other one, even though it may cost us our hides, is a national disease; that is why we find ourselves in our present predicament.

Your Government has probably received a vague answer from Lafragua. I shall fill in the gaps by telling you that since there is a complete lack of funds and troops and since the Government can offer no other aid than that of passing laws, there is a plan to appoint a single Commander-in-Chief for all those states from Coahuila to Sinaloa[47] and New Mexico so as to unify the defense of the frontiers. This plan has been submitted to S. A. for his approval. It has also been suggested to him that Filisola be made commander. Government officials themselves, however, doubt that he will be approved for this post because of the long-standing enmity between the two men. In any event it is certain that your Government will turn to S. A., at the same time hampering him in the matter of men and weapons. When you want something else from the federal Government it will be absolutely imperative to submit a plan that I can support. But I must have instructions, for I repeat that the business of getting *pledges* is only a stopgap method. It is also imperative that we put aside all undue complacence, remembering that this can be purchased only by bloodshed and the fate of our fellow citizens.

47 Both are northern states of Mexico.

You will receive in the next mail a treatise on the excise tax bill which you gentlemen seem to have put through without opposition. In order to lend more weight to my arguments, I availed myself of your letter and last night had a talk with Lafragua. He assured me that a decree proclaiming the abolition or suspension of the tax would be issued today. Everybody says that a great deal of rascality has been involved in this matter and that the Minister has realized several thousand pesos from the deal. Because of this as well as on account of other little matters, the Minister will soon announce his resignation. But it will come too late, because there is no doubt that he has *secretly* terminated the famous parleys over the English debt, thereby plunging us into the bottomless pit of misery. He is the one who carried on the wild, filthy deals undertaken by Don Luis de la Rosa and as a result has left us much worse off. He went through with the whole business without taking the President into his confidence. The President, however, has begun to have his secret suspicions of the man, although undoubtedly he knows less about the situation than I do. I ask you to consider this last statement as strictly confidential. Baranda is being considered for the post of Minister of Finance, but he is afraid of taking the job because all the funds have been exhausted. If the states do not make great sacrifices our army will fall to pieces before seeing action, because the troops will soon be destitute of everything.

Give my regards to our friend Castañeda, and encourage him.

(Signed)

Mexico City, November 25, 1846

Sr. Don Francisco Elorriaga

My dear friend:

At last I can tell you that I am a free man. I have resigned my post in the Government of the district. It is a job that will always entail serious trouble and perhaps dangerous commitments for the poor devil who happens to have it. Our friend Don Pedro Anaya is going on as the Mayor and has vowed that he will resign the first of the month.

Those trying situations which I had formerly considered as merely possible have today become more than probable, since with the approaching opening of the sessions the excitement and maneuvering of the political groups increase. They will make their bow before the public and proceed to get into all kinds of fights over the election of the President. Up until three days ago the *puros* were putting Almonte up as their candidate but they have suddenly changed their tactics. Now they are supporting Farías, because they think they are sure to get a majority of votes. I shall not be surprised if they change their minds again. The *moderados* are backing Salas. All this maneuvering should be understood as pertaining to the election of the Vice-president, since both parties have agreed on the election of the President by choosing S. A. It seems that he is looking upon Almonte's candidacy with some degree of hostility and downright hatred. The *puros* say that they can count on a majority of our delegates from Durango, because they are excluding Hernández for his *Decembrist* affiliations. They are already making threats and promising that they will start riots in the city and fights in the galleries of the Chamber if the majority of the delegates show any hesitancy. Yesterday Boves told me about several *coups* that occurred at the preliminary sessions. They included: the seizure of ecclesiastical property; condemnation of Paredes and his Cabinet as Monarchists; banishment of this party; and the expulsion of the Spanish Minister. Boves said he could not recall the fifth point.

In the midst of all this hubbub there fell like a bolt of lightning on a powder keg a news report printed in the *New York Herald* which was circulated very secretly here. It states, on the basis of a letter written here in Mexico City, that S. A. has concluded a secret treaty with the United States. By the terms of the treaty he has promised to hand over to that country the states that have been invaded, or at least parts of them. He will arrange matters in such a way that our troops will offer only a token resistance, so that after a few defeats our country will feel inclined to accept any kind of peace settlement. As a reward for carrying out these commitments the U. S. guarantees S. A. the Presidency for ten years, during which time the territorial divisions will be arranged so that these lands can easily be incorporated into the American confederation. Ultimately its flag would wave uncontested over the entire continent. All these details were to have been printed in today's *Republicano,* but time was pressing and the news was deferred until tomorrow. The whole thing looks like a Cabinet intrigue designed to divide us, and especially to discourage us in our efforts to continue the war; because once a lack of confidence in our Commander has been aroused the disintegration of the army would be a foregone conclusion. After this would come the peaceful occupation of the country by the enemy. But even if there were something of the truth in the report, we could gain nothing by giving it full credence. We have therefore agreed to take all possible advantage of the incident by using it to force S. A.'s hand and make him carry on to the end. That is the complexion the situation is assuming, as you will find out in the next mail. Therefore, keep this affair secret and do not confide in irresponsible persons. Be careful not to believe everything you are told, because you will certainly get more news in this mail and it will probably be exaggerated. We are in the midst of a terrible crisis.

I cannot be pleased with you if you have consented to my election as senator, because I do not think I am mistaken in saying that, if you have, it must have cost you more trouble than if you had tried to prevent it. In the latter case you could have counted on several capable collaborators. . . . I shall omit the *perhaps* in order to restore the thought to its true meaning. I want you to know that my election has caused me such misery that I do not know what to do with myself. I do not share the sentiments of those persons who have taken it upon themselves to make Durango happy. Guided by this conviction, a very melancholy one for him who suffers from its effects, I made up my mind several days ago not to take any part in future plans for that district, preferring to let myself be carried along by the tide of events. A long succession of disappointments and difficulties has kept me from completely abandoning that part of the country in which I was born, although you know that I have more than enough reason to do so.

I can continue this no longer. Goodbye.

(Signed)

Say something on my behalf so that I may be considered when the question of the compulsory loan comes up.

Mexico City, December, 1846

My dear friend:

To praise good deeds and to give credit to their authors is not only an act of Justice due them; it is an obligation imposed by society and by the fine encouragement such a course provides for those individuals dedicated to public service. It was because of these principles and my affection for Durango that I took pen in hand and wrote the article that you will read in today's *Republicano*. I also felt that by so doing I could impose a certain punishment upon myself and thus make amends for those outbursts of ill humor that I could not repress in my previous letter. In this article you will find the opinion you asked me for concerning the imminent reform of the constitution. Others will find the article an act of justice which they could not expect, at least from me, for they actually had no right to expect such a thing from me. Do not tell people that I wrote the article. Tell them that someone else wrote it. In this way it may be effective, and you will be able to get impartial opinions about it. After that you can do anything you see fit. Two gross errors slipped into the first and third paragraphs in the second column: the typesetter put *potico* for *político* and *escusiones* for *concusiones*.

The preliminary sessions have started, and up to today the *puros* have been able to count on the support of two-thirds of the members. Their opponents are desperate, because they are sure they can control the Congress if all members are there; but there own followers are absent. The sixth[48] is going to come, and with it the election of President and Vice-president. This will settle more than one point of vital importance. The *moderados* are inclined toward a plan that no one knows the outcome of. They intend to stay away from the sessions of the Congress until their representatives arrive. In this way they think they can prevent the elec-

48 Congress was to convene officially on December 6 and would elect the President and Vice-president. Although this letter is undated it must have been written in the first days of December.

tion planned by the others. None of the others has come to any definite conclusions about this matter.

Yesterday I received an invitation from Rejón to have a conference with him, and we met later in the day. From his very first words he made it clear what he wanted to speak to me about. "We want you to enlist under our banners," he said. "You would then serve in the high position to which your ability calls you, or you *would unite* with us if we lose." I admit to you that I was quite impressed by this sort of direct language as well as by the frank, ingenuous explanation he gave about the principles his party proposes to carry on to victory. He left nothing for me to wish for or to hesitate about. His goal seems to me to be set too high, and I am afraid that this time we shall lose because we shall be attempting too much. Mankind cannot realize that too much light is blinding. I found a good excuse to get out of the dilemma without solving it, because fortunately he explained to me that in order for his plans to succeed, I would have to stay here in Mexico City for a long time. I did not wish to learn any more, since what I already knew seemed exaggerated. At that moment I repented *for the third time* that I had refused the offers which you had repeatedly presented me to accept membership in the delegation.[49] Unfortunately, I am the sort of man who, although he becomes discouraged from time to time, never quite loses all hope.

Your bones have been rattling considerably in the combinations being formed for the election of Vice-president. The time has come for me, too, to enlarge my perspective of things, and I find that it is also a question of considering some grave sins, because I lied shamelessly when I attempted to express my estimation of your value. Perhaps there will never come a time when I can be convinced and I shall therefore experience regrets without, however, failing to be happy over it.

Triguero refused to head the government of the Federal District.

They have finally set aside the forced loan,[50] for as was to be expected it produced only discredit and annoyance and no money. The news appearing in today's *Republicano,* taken from the *Monitor,*[51] is not correct, according to what I was told by ex-Minister Iturbe. He was one of the money lenders involved and he said that the clergy were accepting the drafts openly and frankly.

I shall have to terminate my letter at this point so that I can busy myself with more disagreeable and difficult tasks. As a result of the decree issued by Olaguível ordering the seizure of the Duke of Monteleone's possessions as the property of the nation, the Spanish Minister has sent in a strong protest. When the question was passed on to the Council for deliberation, this body appointed me a member of a special commission to make a report, and the Minister of Foreign Affairs insists that the question

49   As a deputy to the national Congress.
50   Levied on the clergy in October to the amount of two million pesos.
51   Newspaper in Mexico City.

be settled by early tomorrow. And it is already half-past eight in the evening! Now to work.

Goodbye.

(Signed)

Lafragua has sweetened the bitter pill for me by repeating his assertion that the business on the 8th was finished, as you requested in your previous communication. Only you people there can know whether this is true or not.

I am taking a few more minutes to tell you that the *illiterate element* there is *lacking in manners*. Why didn't you accord me a little praise for having assumed the halo that belongs to a keen and discriminating author? Have my notes to Prescott seemed so impertinent and silly? I was hoping that I could find sympathy even among the common people who have caused me to do so many foolish things. All that remains now is for the author to get angry and give me a sound shaking.

Mexico City, December 23, 1846[52]

Señor Don Francisco Elorriaga
My dear friend:

You owe this letter to the fact that you were defeated in the Congress, for if you had come out as the President-elect I had made up my mind that I would not fling my sword into the balance. You ran in competition with General S. A. and you lost because of the defection of two men who had committed themselves to support you.[53] As your friend I am infinitely happy over the whole thing. It would have been really impossible for you to stay in office by peaceful means, because you would have had a hand-to-hand struggle with *puros* and sympathizers of S. A.; and you could not have relied upon the help of the *moderados* in view of the fact that they are not united. I was all for having you chosen as Vice-president and I believe that in that capacity you would have accomplished much good; but your sponsors deserted you for Ocampo,[54] and this is certainly due to the fact that they lost heart during the election proceedings. I am convinced that you would have offered Farías good competition, but only the representatives from Durango held their ground. There was no one to lead them, and as I supposed all along Rejón had no one that he could put up.

A peculiar circumstance has forced me to remain away from home. I write these lines at the home of my companion, Guerrero, where I have taken refuge. Twenty emissaries sent by Farías are looking for me to force

52 From December 23 to February 10 the Americans and the Mexicans prepared for their battle in northern Mexico, and Scott was preparing for his invasion of Veracruz. The main preoccupation of the Mexican Government was trying to raise money to finance the war.
53 Santa Anna received eleven votes and Elorriaga nine.
54 Melchor Ocampo was one of the prominent liberal leaders of the century. He received eight votes.

me to take the job of Minister of Foreign Affairs. Does this not amaze you? Here I am, speculating on the man's impatience and hoping that I shall be able to escape by making myself invisible tonight, because I have firmly made up my mind not to be made a clown of. For the first time I have had the feeling of apprehension for the present and for the future, since anyone who knows how irritable and peremptory he can be will understand that he is a man who cannot be scorned with impunity, nor can one go along with him in perfect harmony. What shall I do tomorrow? I have no political party on which to lean, and without this support a Minister cannot continue in office.

Yesterday they adopted an infamous method of annulling your candidacy. When the session was about to begin Perdigón circulated a pamphlet attacking you. At today's session I had another pamphlet passed around, a copy of which I am enclosing in this letter. I am not sending you any additional copies, because, as I have said, I am a fugitive from my own home. I did not think it wise to include any details, because I wanted to maintain the unity of impression that I planned to present. Furthermore, I do not believe my statements need amplification, this method being characteristic of those who adopt guerrilla tactics. I repeat that I am glad for your sake that we do not need your help. The political situation is horrible and of such a nature that a description of it cannot be entrusted to writing.

The news I get from Durango is causing me profound worry, because I see that our friend Castañeda did not do what he should have done to prevent the reaction. Later he even gave it effective assistance. I think that by the time you get this letter you will have already understood a phrase of mine about which you asked me for a quick, clear explanation. I did not give it to you, hoping that others would take it upon themselves to give it in sufficiently significant terms. The illness is grave and urgent and is one of those critical situations that demand a stroke of genius to prevent its results. It is one that has borne the marks of its origin ever since it was in the fetus stage. The mistake was made at election time and was later made legal by the imprudent protection given by our Government to certain persons who seek to discredit it and who, in my opinion, are betraying it now or will betray it later on. Your situation reminds me of the one in 1825, and I am afraid that the similarity may be perfect and especially more fraught with evil consequences, since you do not have a Don Santiago Baca at your side.

I must say something about your fulminating letter in which you rake me over the coals. Do you think you made me angry? Well, if you do you are badly mistaken, because at least in so far as you yourself are concerned, your letter left me highly pleased and satisfied. In spite of your reaction I insist on performing my task, and for that reason I must tell you that you are either losing your former skill or are making no progress. The press in the capital has published accounts of public events in which I have figured, events about which the newspapers in Durango have maintained a stubborn silence—in Durango, whose governments and people I have served, if not well, then at least faithfully and loyally. What proof of their esteem have they given me? What encouragement has there been to go on serving them? You can probably guess. These are *facts,* and I mention them so that you may realize you were wrong in reproaching me. The truth of the matter is that people are afraid of the good reputation I might acquire among the men of my own section of the country. Nothing is being published in my favor that might make a contrast with what is being said to my disadvantage in the groups of hangers-on. In this way it is hoped to keep me forever in obscurity, and therefore any ambition I might have could be satisfied with the little honors that I could be accorded there. Since I am fully aware of this situation, which you understand clearly but are unwilling to discuss with me, I have adopted a contrary course: I am eulogizing those who are trying to humiliate me and am giving them to understand that my intentions are good. I always speak of Durango and its citizens as the best in the world. If these eulogies could lead to the Presidency for any of them, I would be gratified to act in an humble role, because I have always acted upon the principle of *the honor and greatness of my own native district.* This is the only thing that men who come from there are expected to do. When I have deceived myself into thinking that I cannot do anything to add to its glory, I shall have condemned myself to obscurity and have wandered far from home.

You have wrung a confession from me, and I ask you to keep it to yourself, for if I have made such a confession it has been merely to satisfy you. I make no complaint against you, because you have suffered a great deal and you will go on suffering by defending me. I refer to others whom you know better than I do.

Enough of this chatter. I shall put an end to this by rejoicing over the fact that you have received the honor of the Presidency without suffering the sharp pricks of its poisoned thorns.

Goodbye.

Private Correspondence
of the Minister
of Foreign Affairs,
Government and Police

National Palace

Mexico City, December 26, 1846

Sr. Don Francisco Elorriaga
My dear friend:

Here I am, Minister of Foriegn Affairs, much to the alarm of the *puros,* the amazement of the *moderados,* the astonishment of the *monarquistas* and my own despair.[55] Such a singular occurrence of course has its history, but I

55 Hutchinson states that many were astonished because the Cabinet was so moderate. Hutchinson, *Gómez Farías,* 720.

have no time in which to relate it. I am withholding comment until a later occasion, and this letter must serve only as a sort of announcement and suggestion.

Some people here are still making efforts to harass me with the charge that I am a Monarchist, and I would like to have you take this information as a basis for getting your official Government newspaper to dedicate an article in my defense. It can do so by relying upon what the members of the Government and my friends know about my conduct and principles from the time the *Tiempo*[56] started publication.

See to it that the article does not turn out to be only a trifling thing. Take care that it is written by someone with a sense of propriety, for anything written under constraint never achieves its purpose. Otherwise, I would prefer that nothing be said.

Tell Lehemann that his letters have reached me at a time when I do not even have the leisure in which to eat. Have him wait a little longer. My work is so heavy that I am the only one remaining in my office, while the President and his Cabinet members have gone to the famous concert tonight.

Say something to Ursulita and Don Germán to calm and console them. They are probably quite upset over the news of my rashness in accepting the post of Minister. You can pacify them until I get time to write. Give my best regards to my other friends.

I have changed somewhat my usual manner of signing letters. I do this in the hope that you may be caused less embarrassment.

Ramírez

56 Newspaper in Mexico City. Its first issue was January 24, 1846.

CHAPTER IV

CIVIL WAR IN MEXICO CITY

Private Correspondence
of the Minister
of Foreign Affairs,
Government and Police

National Palace

Mexico City, January 13, 1847

Sr. Don Francisco Elorriaga

My dear friend:

Since the greater evil swallows up the lesser, I have been unable to keep from laughing when I think how seriously I took your complaints and troubles and compare them with the ones that are overwhelming me now. I am faced with the greatest risk that a nation and a statesman can face, because the problem is nothing less than that of the fate of the country and the citizen to whom the safety of the country has been entrusted. The copy of the law[1] that I am sending you and the innumerable comments on it that you will receive in later dispatches will impress upon your mind the critical nature of the situation. There is a general feeling of panic, and as was to be expected I am the center of attention, since everyone presumes that upon me depends the fate of our unhappy country. They base this presumption on the fact that they do not believe that I went into this thing blindly. From this they deduce that I have some grand design under way. They are right in many respects and yet they are exaggerating quite a bit. But I do not think that they can guess what I am planning. Consequently, I shall tell you not to believe what may be said to you, because I myself am not at all sure just what course I shall pursue, although I naturally am certain of what I want.

Since I have decided to go on, or, rather, to let myself be dragged along by the stream of events without offering any more than the minimum of resistance to keep from drowning before my time, I do not want to discuss with all of you the manner in which you ought to conduct yourselves under these circumstances. I have likewise said nothing to our deputies, who have consistently shown a hostile attitude toward me as Minister. The absolute freedom of action that I have allowed all of you, a freedom that I respect, is given due consideration in every one of my plans, because it is a question in which each man must act according to the dictates of his

---

1 Ramírez refers to the law passed on January 11 which granted the executive the power to raise fifteen million pesos by mortgaging or selling church property. However, religious, charitable, and educational activities of the clergy were exempted. The law in many ways was a compromise. Some, such as Rejón, wanted to nationalize the church lands. The money of course was to be used in support of the war.

conscience and as a result of his own convictions. Read the circular that I have sent today to your Government and use your influence to have it made public immediately. I request only one thing: Do not tolerate any disturbances nor give occasion for them to occur. Get the Government to conduct itself with dignity and decorum, whichever side it is on. Otherwise it may find itself in a frightful predicament.

Ursulita expressed to me her desire to come here. Go to see her and tell her to wait until the trouble here is over. Tell her and the other members of my family not to worry. The crisis is a terrible one. It is so bad that no one has had the courage to face it. That is why we find ourselves in this wretched state of affairs. I have accepted the situation with all its consequences and I am calm, because even if the worst thing that we can imagine happens, we shall always gain by it. You will see.

It will be to your advantage to know that the law was passed with S. A.'s agreement and at his urgent request, since he had indicated that he was determined to uphold it. Will he? Whether he does or not, I shall at any rate attain my purpose.

Since several difficulties arose in connection with the publication of this law, which was proclaimed at noon today, its opponents took heart by maintaining that the delay was due to weakness on the part of the Government, and the church prebendaries immediately refrained from performing the duties of their office. The news spread, giving it the character of an interdict, but Señor Farías requested the Undersecretary of Justice to ask the Vicar of the order for an explanation. The Vicar replied that this action was the sole responsibility of the prebendaries, who were afraid that there might be some sort of disturbance, as a result of which some persons might get into the church and desecrate it. But he added that for his part he would make no change either in the Cathedral or in the diocese, since he had already given orders that religious functions be continued. As a result of this statement, a notice has been sent to the Dean of the order informing him that he is not to do anything out of the ordinary. The understanding is that if he does not comply with this order the proper steps will be taken against him and all the prebendaries in conformity with the law.

The chief officers of the National Guard unit, the only one now in the city, have come to announce that they are prepared to support the Government. We shall see how this situation turns out. It is one to cause concern, and I would like to have you with me to determine whether it is so very much more worth while to put up with the rather ungrateful criticisms that grow out of one's candidacy for President than to face the obstacles put in my path as a Minister. At least, I would think twice before making a choice.

The Dean's reply has been received. He is quite humble and declares that he will obey orders and that services will go on without hindrance.

It is half-past nine at night, and there is nothing more of special interest to write about. Regards to my family and friends. Goodbye.

(Signed)

Private Correspondence
of the Minister
of Foreign Affairs,
Government and Police

Mexico City, January 16, 1847[2]

Sr. Don Francisco Elorriaga

Dear friend:

This will be the last letter I shall write in the office of the Ministry. Don Mariano Otero, who has declared himself the protector of the special church courts, etc., has been acting in collusion with a certain Parada and has made charges against me, because in order to suppress the disturbances on the 14th[3] I ordered the ringleaders to be remanded to the ordinary courts without distinction as to special privileges.[4] I have also been accused of breaking the law that permits political meetings, which I considered as disturbances.

The Congress handed over the matter to a commission of *moderados,* and this commission decided that it should go to the jury. I have written my resignation which I am going to present to Señor Farías immediately, because I am not inclined to become the plaything of a group of cowards who cannot do anything but raise an outcry from their easy chairs in Congress. No human power will ever get me back again into this irksome job.

Goodbye.   (Signed)

Office of the
Private Secretary
of the Commanding General
of the Liberal Republican Army

San Luis Potosí, January 19, 1847

His Excellency Don José Fernando Ramírez

Esteemed friend and Sir:

I received your welcome letter dated the 13th of this month and I am very favorably impressed with your firm decision to sacrifice in the service of your country all that a man holds most dear in life. For eleven years I have had the satisfaction of knowing your wholesome opinions and the patriotic ideas that you so deeply cherish. From the very first I have professed friendship with you and the respect that ought to be accorded virtue, and it gratifies me to realize that you are not acting contrary to your principles, nor are you forsaking your ideals of loyalty and patriotism.

2   Text states 1846, undoubtedly a misprint.
3   Ramírez refers to the disturbances which took place on the 14th after the law on church lands was officially published by the Farías Government.
4   The question involved is one of which courts, either the special ecclesiastical courts which the clergy had or the regular state courts. Ramírez felt that those involved in the disturbances should be tried in the state courts.

I have been pained at the way the Government has kept silent about the statements that keep pouring from the opposition newspapers—statements criticizing the army and myself. They are so bold as to confuse us with traitors because, as they maintain, we are doing nothing, when everyone knows that the army's inactivity is due to the state of wretchedness and neglect in which it has been kept. This in turn has resulted in a lack of means for giving the army the mobility it needs. Please use the official government journal to contradict these slanders, silencing these writers to whom I am referring, since the Government is thoroughly cognizant of our situation. The truth of the matter is that the army frightens the revolutionists because it is restraining them and upsetting their plans for insurrection and chaos. Hence the unjust attacks leveled against it.

See that you keep in good health. This is the wish of your true friend,

Antonio López de Santa Anna

Mexico City, February 10, 1847[5]

Sr. Don Francisco Elorriaga

My dear friend:

Do not feel bad about being on the losing side in the voting on the law promulgated the 14th of last month. You have always been able to get a great deal done, although one always hopes to accomplish everything. This has never happened, nor will it happen in the future, because in the lives of men and nations there are certain opportunities which come once and, if lost, never come again. If it is possible for the Government to procure sufficient funds (which I doubt) it cannot do so for at least twenty days, and by that time the money won't do any good. The way I look at it the question has already been definitely settled, except for a miracle, which we do not have the right to expect, since Providence has already granted us too many favors.

Our present administration continues in office because there is no one who wants to overthrow it. There is no such individual because no one knows what to do after having seized power. Farías has had more than one opportunity to get fearful revenge and yet he has stubbornly refused. The *puros* finally made up their minds to treat him as the Scottish Rite Masons had treated Guerrero.[6] And who do you suppose came to his aid? The *moderados*. They offered to support him on condition that they could organize the Ministry and that he [Farías] would consent to follow blindly

5   It can probably be said that from February 10 to April 2 Mexico lost the war. On February 22-23 the battle of Buena Vista took place, and though it can hardly be called a victory for Taylor it certainly forced Santa Anna to retreat, thus opening all of northern Mexico to the Americans. On March 9 Scott landed near Veracruz and on the 29th of the same month he occupied the city. Preparations were then begun for the invasion of eastern Mexico. In Mexico City in this period a revolt, described by Ramírez in his letter of April 2, resulted in the removal of Gómez Farías from the Government.

6   In other words, get rid of him.

the voting of their majority, meanwhile being satisfied with merely a *token leadership*. He has made the serious mistake of refusing their offer, fancying that he can control the situation. The puppet would have died if the strings had been pulled by a different hand.

Turning to another matter, I can tell you that the behavior of the Durango authorities has not caused me any pain, because I was expecting it.[7] The only exception was in certain details which could not be foreseen and which give rise to unfavorable impressions. I do not think that it was necessary for the committee and the Government to speak with such bitterness, which formed a striking contrast with the measured language used by the Bishop. Under the circumstances, I do not believe that it was the wise thing to take such a determined stand against the Government as a whole by flinging down the gauntlet in a gesture of real defiance, when the same result could have been obtained by other means. Today such actions take on the hue given them by political and religious passions. But you know how short-lived such passions are in our country, even though the reactions are terrible. The storm that holds us now in its grip has not been heavy enough to prevent us from seeing clearly that the principles enunciated by the Durango government present obstacles to the development of our system. Since these principles have been announced at the very time that Olaguível is ordering all his subordinates to disregard any order coming from the federal authorities, and at the time when he is seizing private property by virtue of his position as Governor and is threatening with force anyone who demands payment in return, you will readily imagine what is being said by those who want something more *solid* than a republic, and even by republicans themselves. I give thanks again and again to those inexperienced men who provided me with a just and honorable opportunity to give up my seat as Minister!

At present I am having to deal with these men and their abominable intrigues and that is why I have nothing new to tell you, because you no doubt already know how the comedy is going to end. The jury informed me that I would not be permitted to attend the discussions to answer to the charges against me in that body, and consequently I indicated that I would give up all idea of offering a defense. This gave Otero the chance to get down to personalities by heaping insults upon me. The public has brought its own judgment against the man who abused the privileges of his office to insult one who had not heard the charges nor had been able to defend himself. The opinion that I had held about the matter from the very first was confirmed.

In one of your letters you tell be about the feeling of disappointment you have noticed among your friends because of the silence I have maintained in connection with my senatorship. They have considered this silence as a slight against them. Perhaps I was the only one who could

7 Durango, along with a number of other states, suspended publication of the law of January 11 and protested to Congress.

complain about such a feeling, in accordance with parliamentary practices. You know that it is customary to call upon an individual when he is absent, whether or not there is any need for his presence. That was not what was done in my case, and you are also aware of how far I could let my imagination take me in that event. Since my family arrived safely today, I shall not be able to carry out the proposal hinted at in my last letter. And now that this incident has come up to block my way, it will not be a bad idea to weather the storm on the high seas themselves. You know that I am something of a fatalist. I shall not be idle. Rather I shall be very busy, and you will share in the fruits of my labors.

I want some frank, honest advice from you. Shall I send in my resignation? The only thing I am not sure about is just how it will be received. You ought to know. This time I am not guided by any kind of political considerations. The only thing I am being guided by is the obvious impossibility of discharging my duties. Shall I return immediately to private life with my family?

The first letter in which you recommended that I give some attention to the case of Don Pedro García Conde reached me when I had already given up my Cabinet post. Consequently I was unable to do anything, because for several days I had felt obliged to go into hiding to escape the demands made upon me by the President and other individuals who were trying to get me to take up my duties again. I have been in retirement ever since that time.

It is time for the mail to be collected, and there is still a great deal I might write.

(Signed)

Confidential   Mexico City, April 2, 1847

My dear friend:

Although the interruption in our correspondence must have kept you in a state of uncertainty and apprehension, I believe that you will be amply repaid by what I can tell you now, because by viewing events that have almost reached their conclusion you will be able to judge them accurately. When a person writes under pressure of immediate events it is easy for him to let his emotions get the better of him, even though he tries to maintain the strictest impartiality. But the reverse is true when these events are examined in perspective. That is the way I can look at them at the present moment, and I tell you with a heavy heart that everyone, everyone without exception, behaved in such a manner that we richly deserve the scorn and derision of all cultured peoples. We are nothing, absolutely nothing. An additional aggravating detail is that our stupid vanity makes us believe that we are really all-important. Our people have a superabundance of vanity. I myself am greatly to blame, too, because I have encouraged it, although with the best intentions. You will therefore be rendering me a real service by keeping my letter confidential, since you no doubt have an idea of what the consequences would otherwise be. Let us get down to the main point, as you request in your letter to which this one is an answer.

The press has probably informed you that the written statements, maneuvers and behavior of the *moderado* party have completely nullified the laws of the 11th of January and the 4th of February,[8] and in this way they have made it absolutely impossible for the government to get the necessary funds to help our troops. At the same time they were actively fomenting the disgraceful *Polkos* revolution.[9] Farías was unaware of these serious developments and thought that he was about to obtain the fifteen million-odd pesos and even more. He never even thought that a revolution would be attempted. I was of a different opinion and as a result I did what little I could to get his friends to induce him to resign before the revolution broke out, for such proof would compel him to quit. All this happened about two or three weeks before the insurrection got started, and I know that *puros*, *moderados* and *santanistas*[10] did everything in their power to get him to resign, but all they accomplished was to irritate him still more.

In this state of affairs it was imperative to resort to violent measures, and it is only just to say that this decision was made by his own party. The *puros* decided to settle the whole matter by having the Legislature declare him incompetent. The *moderados* were opposed and declared themselves Farías's protectors, as you have probably read in the *Republicano*, which made such a big affair out of the silly incident. There was no element of patriotism or policy in their opposition. It was simply a party move to put their opponents in a false light and thereby take over control. Affairs moved on their course; Farías, determined to carry out the law, struggled against overpowering resistance, since neither Government employees nor private individuals wanted to serve a tottering government. Meanwhile, the Independence Battalion started an absurd uprising. Farías had thoughtlessly offended the men, stirring them up by his order for them to be on the march to Veracruz within twenty-four hours. Since the Battalion is composed of skilled workers, small tradesmen, lawyers and so forth, you will understand why they found it quite simple to rebel against a government that antagonizes them.

The frightful lack of initiative shown by the Congress during these developments ought to have produced an open break, since by its refusal to grant the Government any funds it forced the latter to go on with the

---

8   The law of February 4 was to get around some of the complications of the law of January 11. It allowed the Government to raise five million pesos immediately.

9   The text states "polcos." Ramírez continues with the story of the revolt, which began on February 27. The name *Polkos* was given to that part of the national guard recruited from the upper classes because they enjoyed dancing the polka.

10   Supporters of Santa Anna.

execution of the laws already in effect. At the same time the Congress was putting more and more obstacles in the way of enforcing these laws, increasing the irritation among opponents by the violent quarrels that occurred daily in the legislative Chamber. The deputies called one another "traitors," "obstinate fools," "corrupt villains," etc., terms which were bandied around in true schoolboy fashion. Members of the clergy, who had been spying about, dealing in hatreds and fears, seized the opportune moment I have referred to to open their money chests and start a civil war at the very time the foreign enemy was casting anchor in Veracruz harbor. The Treasury, which they had declared exhausted when it was a matter of defending the nation and the faith which these clergymen represent, was found to be full to overflowing when it came to killing Mexicans. The revolution broke out, and there were plenty of funds to finance uprisings, while the Government and the few troops that were supposed to have made the bloody catastrophe at Veracruz an impossibility were eating their meagre little loaves. Eleven days after the shooting started, that is, on the 9th of March, the revolutionists had 93,000 pesos in their coffers after paying all their expenses, which were phenomenal.

Once hostilities had begun it was no longer proper for Farías to resign. I shall go even further and say that he could not. It would have looked like a well-deserved punishment for his imprudence and obstinacy, and in addition the newly created institutions would have been without any support whatever in the endless chain of insurrections. He realized his duty at this point and he discharged it with such dignity and valor that he made even his enemies admire him, winning not a few friends and admirers from their ranks. Farías, deprived of all support, with a handful of public men about him, struggled against the most powerful and influential classes of society, fighting against the Congress itself and reduced to the last extremity, never for a moment became untrue to himself nor evinced the slightest indication of weakness. He faced the storm that might have destroyed him but which could not make him surrender. We have to admire a man like that, for whom we could wish only a little more good judgment in choosing a cause to espouse and the propitious moment to carry it through. During this time there came the reaction in Congress which you have heard about, with the deputies engaged in fighting among themselves, with protests as weapons. The *moderados* clamored for a session of Congress to help the revolutionists get out of their fight. The *puros* were against it because they foresaw that if the session did not, as they were sure it would, result in Farías's resignation, at the least he would be deprived of the few means of defense which he had left, since new obstacles would be placed in his path. All this will explain the behavior of the deputies and also the horrible indifference with which they received the news of the disembarkation of the Americans. The contestants preferred to lose their country if they could only keep their jobs.

The scapularies, medals and bits of cloth and bags of relics that hung by the dozen around the necks of the revolutionists, particularly of those soft, idle youths who make up our socially elite, would have caused anyone unacquainted with our customs to think that he was in a camp of martyrs of the Faith; he would have believed that all these men would be capable of sacrificing him for the preservation of their religion, stricken by the impious laws that permitted the seizure of church property. It was soon understood that the display was an evidence of weakness and that all this parade of scapularies was an out-and-out act of coquettishness encouraged by the innocent devotion of the nuns and the mercenary beliefs of the clergy. Affection reaped an abundant harvest in that devout business.

That this was the case was revealed by the events which occurred, as I recall, between the 13th and the 14th. They took place as a result of the change which was made in the plan for rebellion. The revolutionists saw with astonishment that the people were not siding with them as they had expected. The people remained indifferent to the cry about religion; despite the speeches made by several churchmen in the different sections of the city during the first few days, they either took no part at all or sided with the Government. Added to these circumstances is the fact that the revolutionists themselves were not in complete agreement with the plan, since only a very few were acquainted with it and the rest knew about it only after it was printed.[11] It was drawn up by some persons in the Chapter House of the Cathedral and by Anzorena, under the sponsorship of some convent supervisors.

This schism grew to the point where it gave rise to explanations, which produced the change in the plan. It was reduced to a single article, to get rid of Farías, the sole point on which all had agreed from the beginning. They had come to this agreement first because of their hatred for him, and then later because they feared him. The religious issue was put aside because it no longer served their purpose. When the clergy realized what was going on they became justly alarmed. They likewise took their stand and wanted to compel the rebels by withdrawing their funds unless they included nullification of the laws[12] in the plan. The revolutionists refused and a scene ensued in which the clergy and the Bishop suffered the most degrading humiliation: that of seeing their Archbishop and the Dean of the Metropolitan District held up to dirision by *Don Simplicio's* wretched editors.

Money for the troops being unavailable, Payno[13] had an interview with Irizarri.[14] The latter received him with expressions of sympathy, and after some melancholy and painful remarks in which conscience played a leading part, Irizarri told him that in view of the fact that blood had al-

11   The text states ". . . los demás rompieron cuando estaba impreso." But in Riva Palacio, *México a través de los siglos*, IV, 634, it is ". . . los demás lo supieron etc." Obviously the former is a misprint.
12   The laws of January 11 and February 4.
13   Manuel Payno was a moderate liberal.
14   The Archbishop.

ready begun to flow copiously, the clergy could not give even a single peso because of the fear of doing something *irregular*. You can well imagine the effect that all this talk had on a hungry revolutionist, a desperate man who found himself thus deserted when his mission was only half accomplished. "Let us put aside all hypocritical talk, Your Reverence," said Payno. "See what you can do to help us get out of our predicament. If it is irregularity that you fear, nothing can be done about it now, and you would be doing nothing more irregular than what you are doing at present by permitting blood to be shed. You are the ones who fomented this revolt and kept it going with the funds you provided for it. You are the ones who have caused the bloodshed." Payno ended by saying that if by noon that same day the money he had requested were not furnished to the battalions engaged in the revolt, with the exception of those from Victoria, Hidalgo and, I believe, Mina, they would abandon their barracks and march to Tacubaya to submit to the Government, thereby leaving the clerics to depend upon help from the *Polkos*. The revolution certainly would have ended that day if the cautious ecclesiastics at the Chapter House had had more power. But before noon the money was handed over to the revolutionists, with the promise of support to the end, and the civil war was prolonged. The clergy could not get their champions to demand the repeal of the laws, and in order not to lose out completely they agreed that in the proclamation announcing the amended plan Farías should be called "irreligious."[15]

The revolution has been useful only to General S. A. He was more fortunate than Napoleon returning from Russia, because he was able to come back without an army and still be certain that he would be received as an angel of peace and comfort. The political parties disputed over which one would receive him with most acclaim, and even the women went to work making garlands to strew in his path. The road from Mexico City to Querétaro was thronged with carriages filled with people of all classes and financial means coming out to welcome him and win his favor. Even the Congress, disregarding the strictness of its *regulations,* appointed a committee to go to Guadalupe and receive his oath of office. The *inflexible moderados* calmly consented to let all the members of the Congress leave to attend the ceremonies, and Otero as President of the Congress was up to his old tricks again, trying to get himself appointed on the committee. In spite of the bitter speeches that were made against the measure, representing it as an act of shameful degradation, Otero himself voted for it, and at midnight amid the pealing of bells, salvos of artillery, fireworks, etc., the committee from Congress left for Guadalupe. On the following day the members of the Cabinet, together with Rejón and a committee of *puros,* went there to congratulate the Spirit of Peace[16] on behalf of the

15 The new plan was published on March 9.
16 Santa Anna. Mecham claims that on March 29, 1847, Santa Anna had issued a decree revoking the law of January 11, in return for a cash payment of two million pesos from the clergy. J. Lloyd Mecham, *Church and State in Latin*

Government. Everyone entered the contest to gain his favor and indulgence, since the balance of victory between the *Polkos* and the *puros* depended upon which side of the scales he would cast his sword.

We did not have to wait long for the disillusionment, nor was it difficult to predict what would happen. I knew beyond a doubt that S. A.'s sympathies were for the *puros*. I must admit, incidentally, that this was very just, because they have been the party most loyal and helpful to him. But his sympathies could not extend beyond them and still provide him with an honorable way out so as to save him from the mortification of defeat, because the *puros* had been almost overwhelmed by the greater power of the opposition party, with which all the other parties had joined with the single, plain campaign program of "hatred for Farías and the *puros*." The *puros* would not yield without a fight. On the contrary, they wanted complete control and even more: they wanted to make examples of the revolutionists by punishing them, and they wanted to do this quickly and with that lack of sober second thought characteristic of a pure democracy. These pretensions of course brought about an open break, because S. A., in his capacity as a public official, could not accord them this advantage. It was against his own principles and the program he had outlined. To make his position more secure, or at least to make it easier to defend himself, he was constrained to join the more powerful party, even though he was running the risk of delivering himself into the hands of his enemies. This is what he finally did, and he did it in a most determined manner. The rest of his enemies, who are without hope and are lacking in prudence, have put up a fight. Farías, that fanatical politician with the good intentions, said *one day before* S. A.'s entry that the General had come to break up all his plans at the worst possible time, because given *three more days* he could have saved the Republic!

Up to a certain point, the reason for all these misunderstandings was obvious, when one takes into account the state of affairs at the time S. A. arrived. Personal animosities, quarrels and even assassinations that followed the end of hostilities and which you have no doubt heard of through the press, will give you some idea of the fearful excitement and hatred that divided the contending parties. It was impossible, therefore, to maintain a neutral stand between them, and the slightest incident was enough to cause distrust, the prelude to hostilities. The demolition of some of the barricades used by the *puros* before those of the *Polkos* were torn down, the departure for Veracruz of the battalions defending the Government—these and other incidents were the prime motives for the separation, which finally ended in an open break. This break, which also occurred under extraordinary circumstances, came to be personified by Farías's dismissal. But before I discuss this I shall tell you about another

America (Chapel Hill, 1934) 423. He was, as Ramírez describes, then on his way to Mexico City to take over the reins of the Government.

ridiculous and shameful incident; or rather—I do not know how to describe it.

The *Polkos* claimed the victory and from then on they laid plans to humiliate their opponents. For this reason the *moderados* saw to it that they themselves were given the task of guarding the President's Palace. To effect this humiliation they made a long round-about march that resulted in a prolonged ovation. The balconies were bedecked with bunting, the ladies threw down victory crowns of woven flowers, and servants went on ahead of the procession strewing flowers over the streets. The approaches to the Palace were flower-decked, and the members of the Palace guard were showered with flowers. The very stands of arms were covered with flowers and blooming branches. These same demonstrations have been going on every time the *Polkos* guards change posts. But they are not in evidence in the case of the others. I do not know whether it is my inclination to be cautious or my strict sense of propriety that prompts me to view events this way; but these demonstrations make me feel ashamed when I think of the reasons given to justify them. I got angry when I recalled that all this was going on at the very time Veracruz was suffering the horrors of a savage conflict, and was enduring them for the sake of the silly tribute accorded these would-be cavaliers. I was ashamed, too, when I saw that foreigners were observing all this. I thought of the picture they would paint of us and send out on the packet boat that was ready to sail, and the justly-deserved scorn with which not only civilized but even primitive peoples will think of us. Such an ovation for those who deserved twenty-five lashes, because they were not even good enough to be put in a military prison!

The state of war made S. A.'s departure imperative. He did not leave to repel the invasion, for this I believe to be impossible. He left to prevent the Yankees from getting into Mexico City without firing a shot. An insurmountable difficulty presented itself here in the city. Who was left in charge of the Government? Farías could not continue in office, and the stubborn, hard-headed fellow would not resign. Indeed, he planned to go on at the head of affairs. I grant him, and shall always grant him, a pure, unselfish patriotism. But in giving him this compliment it is absolutely necessary to deny any concessions to him on the score of his mental powers, because only a maniac would feed on such absurd pretensions. Several efforts were made to get him to resign; but since none had any more effect than to irritate him, it was felt that he would have to be compelled to resign by some more subtle plan, one that would present fewer difficulties. The plan adopted was that of abolishing the Vice-presidency and replacing the Vice-president with an ad interim President. Although all this was a mere quibbling of terms, the plan was vigorously defended on the grounds that there were essential differences in the two offices. At any rate, something had to be done to save the situation. Desire substituted for reason, and it could be no other way.

While these discussions were going on the various parties were working hard to win the election of the substitute. As far as membership was concerned, these parties were already quite different from what they had been, since from among the ranks of the *puros* and the *moderados* there came forth still a third party, the *santanistas*. The majority of the *moderados* declared themselves the Cabinet party. The *puros* remained simply as the party of the opposition, sometimes strong, sometimes weak, according to the situation. To make a long story short, there was anarchy in the Congress when the attempt was made to abolish the Vice-presidency in order to elect a Vice-president.

Because of the gravity and uncertainty of the issues depending upon it, this election was a delicate and difficult matter. The man elected was supposed to inspire Congress and S. A. with complete confidence; the former in order to get it to increase the powers of the Government, and the latter so that he would have no occasion to fear treachery during his absence. The Vice-president-elect was also supposed to assure the President of absolute agreement in plans and of help in party coordination. Finally it was a question of getting a man who at least would not create distrust among the parties and who would keep the city calm. S. A. chose Don Pedro Anaya, not without some disappointment on the part of his own followers and others, who were afraid that the choice would bring a reaction from their opponents. The *puros*, dominated by Rejón and, lacking a leader, thought only of putting up a candidate who would be worthy of the job but who would be hostile to S. A. Their only thought was to get vengeance, and they chose Almonte. Their plans were so well laid that I can assure you that if they had not acted foolishly they would have won the election. But they made innumerable mistakes. The first and foremost was that they refused to attend the session. In this way they hoped to delay the issuance of the decree abolishing the office of Vice-president. They thought that they could thus embarrass S. A. and that he would leave while the question was still unsettled. This would make possible the return of Farías to his Government post as the only legitimate authority in the absence of S. A. The situation was terrible at that time! But since the plan was not supported with perseverance to the end, all the embarrassment associated with it came down on the heads of its authors. Public opinion declared itself openly against the Congress, and there were open discussions about dissolving it as an insuperable obstacle in the way of the safety of the Republic. S. A. resolutely declared that he would not leave to join the troops if the election were not held or if Almonte were chosen. Since everyone deemed it urgent for S. A. to leave for the front, the opposition found itself overwhelmed and had to give way, thus losing all the advantage it had enjoyed, because meanwhile efforts were being made among the deputies to get them to oppose the election of Almonte. Farías himself declared that he was against Almonte, although at the same time he did not state that he favored his opponent. This new note of disorganization decided the contest.

The session in which this matter was settled became such a shameful and humiliating affair that I cannot understand how the representative system of government ever survived it. The decree was instantly approved, but it was not possible to complete the roll call in order to proceed to the election, since the various lists passed around resulted in different numbers of names. The impatience of the deputies and of the people in the galleries reached a climax when one of the deputies made a certain vehement motion that was loudly applauded by the galleries. Rejón, irritated by the applause, said a few words to stop it and asked that the session be continued in secret. Then the spectators, losing all sense of propriety, drowned out his remarks with cries of "Down with the traitors!" "Down with the rascals!" etc. The President[17] declared the session adjourned and the tumult grew worse. The people in the galleries refused to leave the Chamber and some booed, while others continued to hurl insults, calling the President a "dirty pig" and adding other obscene remarks. This time it was not possible even to appeal to the temporary help of armed force, because as a consequence of an insulting remark made by a *Polko* soldier of the guard to some *puro* deputies the first day that the Victoria Battalion was on guard duty at the Palace, the Congress decided not to have a guard. With such a fight going on the President ordered that the general in command be called to expel the people in the galleries by force. Anaya came into the Chamber and persuaded those in the galleries to leave, threatening them if they did not obey. They did so; but their obedience was the final, humiliating blow to the Congress. The agitators shouted to Anaya that they would obey him but not the "traitors," etc., and they left, booing the Congress and shouting insults. The election was then held in a secret session between eight and nine o'clock last night, Holy Thursday. About midnight Anaya took the oath of office and assumed his duties. I do not recall ever having seen a spectacle that was sadder, more distressing or more foreboding than the one last night. I got the impression that I was witnessing the dying gasps of the nation. I can see that the continuation of the Republic is an inevitable necessity; but I believe that the continuation of the representative system is an impossibility, at least if given free rein. It has fallen into an abyss of infamy and lack of confidence from which it will emerge with difficulty if it continues to go along its beaten path. If it does not change its course considerably, out-and-out despotism is in store for us. That is, granted we keep our country intact.

April 3[18]

Baranda told me that S. A. would leave last night, and acting upon that presumption I avoided seeing the General. Influenced by events, he ad-

17 The President of the Chamber.
18 From April 8 to August 11 Scott began his advance from Veracruz to Mexico City and by the latter date he was near the capital. During this time the

vanced the time of his departure, leaving yesterday afternoon at two o'clock almost without bidding anyone goodbye. He was with his followers who had agreed that Anaya should be put in charge. Leaving them he entered the inner apartments, went downstairs by himself, and got into a waiting coach. Baranda tells me that the scene was particularly touching, that all the bystanders were deeply moved, and that he felt as if he were watching someone bid his final farewell. He added that even S. A.'s opponents shed tears. S. A. disclosed the fact that he had evil presentiments of the future. The reason for his hasty departure is that he wants to get to La Joya[19] in time to fortify it and stop the progress of the Americans. Two hundred carts were sent out yesterday for the purpose of conveying the troops destined for this purpose.

To avoid breaking the thread of this story of revolution I have passed over two events, the one important for the public interest, the other important for my own. The first event involves the outcome of the famous question about the seizure of church property, an outcome that fully revealed the complete inconsistency of the politicians who opposed the seizure and likewise of the interested parties who rejected it, let us say because of conscience and principles. Both obstacles disappeared when their turn came, thus providing a definite, formal sanction for the acts of their persecuted and discredited opponents.

Farías dealt a mortal blow to the public welfare and to his own reputation by his obstinate refusal to resign, because his enemies would later have done the very thing they refused to let him even begin to do.

As soon as it was learned that S. A. had arrived in Querétaro, numerous delegations left here to meet him and defend their respective causes. One of these delegations was sent by the church assembly, which was still hoping for prompt revocation of the famous laws. The delegates returned so disappointed that they were thinking of continuing the civil war by encouraging the pretensions of the revolutionists. But a division had appeared in the ranks of the rebels, and the matter had to be postponed. S. A. entered the city and received ecclesiastical honors in the Cathedral. The ceremony took place despite the fact that the interior of the Cathedral had indicated a state of *half-mourning* since January 14, when we had been declared under a semi-interdict.

The following day the question of funds was brought up in the Congress in the same form that had produced so much trouble before; that is, in the form of a full and extraordinary authorization, with the very notable difference being that this time it was not a matter of four or fifteen, but of *twenty-millions* to be taken from the same forbidden church funds,

Americans, through the British legation, were trying to negotiate a settlement with Santa Anna and almost succeeded in getting peace without having to fight for Mexico City. The Mexicans during the latter part of this period made ready to defend their capital.

19   A narrow and rugged pass located between Jalapa and Perote on the highway from Veracruz to Mexico City.

as you will clearly observe in Articles 2 and 3 of the law of March 28.
Since this discussion arose at the time of parliamentary chaos, it was strange
that many of those who had voted for the laws of January 11 and February
4 voted against the measure, and that everyone who had been opposed to
it before voted for it now. As a result the main features of the measure
were approved the *third time unanimously!* What opinion do you have
about these matters? What hope do we have for the future?

The clergy had repeated to the point of boredom that their protests were
prompted by true conscience and by the fear of severe censure by old and
new church councils. They claimed that they were fighting to maintain
the inviolability of the prebendaries and ecclesiastical freedom. In fact
they said that they were not against the giving of contributions but only
against the *kinds of contributions* demanded, and they protested that they
would not give a penny unless permission had previously been obtained
from Rome. They thus undertook a greater obligation than the one that
had been demanded of them, while at the same time they recognized the
legality of the Government upon which they had previously called down
the curse of God and men, a curse that stained our streets with the blood
of Mexicans while it was opening wide the doors of the Republic to the
foreign enemy. I do not believe that the civil authorities have any right
to be proud and happy now, for by supporting such a cause they had a decided influence on the course of the lamentable events that have resulted.
Where will the authors of these events seek their consolation? They have
given encouragement to the clergy.

General S. A. summoned the church assembly to enter into negotia-
tions, and the latter sent as their representative to talk with him the same
man who had lavished the treasures of the church among the revolutionists.
Consciences were quieted and reproaches silenced, for it was immediately
agreed that two million pesos cash would be given in exchange for the
repeal of the laws which were the cause of the trouble. Two months before
with this sum of money the clergy could have undoubtedly redeemed themselves. They could have saved Veracruz and our nation and at the same
time saved the 300,000 pesos which they used in a civil war, a war which
is going to cost us very dearly. Our clergy, though short-sighted, cannot
possibly be so short-sighted as not to know that the man who repealed that
law can reinstate it, because they explicitly recognized his right to do so.
They cannot fail to realize that after this law was solemnly passed by the
Congress it was repealed as a simple favor or, rather, as a kind of surrender.
The clergy have committed the unpardonable error of preferring to act in
this situation as a vanquished enemy instead of carrying on their dealings
as equals with equals. This is what they could have and should have done
when they were called to an accounting. Then they would have saved
what they ought to have tried to save at all cost: namely, the respect for
their profession and their duties as churchmen; for in all activities respect
is worth more than money. But now they have lost that respect, because

the people have resorted to armed force against them, and it will no longer be a surprise to them to see the churches closed. The church assembly itself finally became aware of its situation. For that reason, although there was a long and serious discussion about a formal interdict, the assembly did not dare to issue it because it was afraid of losing its weapons, which obviously would have been blunted. Not even the latest turn of events has prompted a large attendance at Holy Week celebrations, the first to be held since the beginning of the civil war. I was not aware of yesterday's procession [Good Friday] until I found myself in the midst of it, because it was lost among the groups of vendors selling rattles, figures of Judas, fruit, etc., and the curious bystanders who thronged the plaza and who did not even remove their hats out of respect.

This development, which the false philosophy created by our revolutionists will consider a symptom of social progress, is in my opinion an indication of death and destruction; because, when our people get to the point where they do not believe in anything, they will not respect anything, and it is a fact that no nation can survive when the gallows is the only standard by which the morality of actions is judged. It is true that our religious system, such as it exists today, is absolutely too weak to make our society a moral one, for if we examine it closely and from a philosophical viewpoint, it becomes obvious that Christianity has degenerated into gross idolatry, and that out-and-out ugly polytheism is the only religion of the priesthood and of the people. This is the ultimate, fatal stage of society. It manifests itself among us with the same vices, the same hollowness and the same pestilential scars with which it manifested itself in Greece and Rome, whose weakness grew in proportion as the legions of impotent gods increased in number. The ancient Mexicans had more faith in Huitzilopochtli[20] than we have in Jesus Christ. In spite of their fear and anguish they defended themselves against the intrepid conquistadors in a manner that today makes us ashamed of the war we are waging against a gang of adventurers. The priests of those ancient Mexicans bore arms and perished beneath the ruins of their temples. Well, here I am again, talking about something that is quite far from my original intentions! Let us go on to the other point, which involves me personally.

I had not seen S. A. since 1842, and, although during my brief term as Minister we had some dealings together, these circumstances did not seem to me to warrant my calling on him. At least that is what my feeling of pride prompted me to suppose. Perhaps this feeling was an exaggerated one; but it did not lack a certain degree of dignity. I still had not quite made up my mind, however, when on the 27th of last month I met the Minister of War in one of the corridors of the Palace. Without delay he told me that at the President's request he had been looking for me since the previous day in order to tell me to choose between an assignment to the French

20 God of War.

legation or to the British. I was to consult with him as soon as I had decided what to do. You cannot imagine what a disagreeable surprise this was; S. A. was appropriating my services in quite an unjust manner, however generous and genteel it might seem. It immediately occurred to me that Baranda must be behind all this, and I was disgusted at the way it was done. I reproached him for it, only to discover that he knew nothing about it. Almonte corroborated this. He had been present at the conference at which S. A., who was making plans to put certain individuals into specified public jobs, suggested this business about the legations. Almonte was asked to make me the offer which I learned about later from the Minister of War, since the latter had offered to approach me. Being thus under compulsion there was no alternative but to suffer the embarrassment of an interview, to which Baranda accompanied me. There the same offer was repeated and my prompt decision requested.

I did not see S. A. again for a couple of days. This was because I did not have the courage either to refuse or to accept. On the third day I went to the office of the Minister of Foreign Affairs, where I found a memorandum signed by the President. This decided the matter. Cañedo was assigned to the French legation, Valdivieso to the Spanish, and I got the tremendous job with the English legation. I had a talk with the President in order to make some suggestions, which I hoped would result in a change of plan. But quite the opposite happened, because the President agreed with my suggestions and gave me time and a free choice as to an opportunity for me to go to London and prepare the work which seemed to him to be the requisite preliminaries. Thrown off my guard by this reply, I received the final blow when he told me that if the assigned legation did not suit me, I could choose from among the others the one I preferred, or else I could choose some public office, since he wanted to accommodate me and give me a job that was to my liking. I felt like a simpleton and replied with what had to be and actually was the truth. I said I was not looking for any kind of job and that his regard for me was sufficient compensation. Here I am, with a load on my shoulders that unfortunately I must bear.

My *tacit* agreement, for up to today I have said neither "yes" nor "no," occurred before we received news of the developments in Veracruz, developments which I was hoping would be of some comfort to us—that is, that Veracruz would be able to resist until our troops could unite at a point where they could check the enemy's advance. This would give us the opportunity to prepare a peace which would not be humiliating, even granting that we were defeated. Last minute developments have robbed me of that hope, for I am afraid that we are being beaten ignominiously and that the peace treaty will be signed in Mexico City. In that event I shall not have the courage to appear at the world's leading court.[21] My pride as a Mexican is superior to our degradation. This is all I can say. And my pride will not let me decide to represent a people who through their foolish quarrels, their childish

21 Presumably St. James.

peevishness, and their lack of common sense have not even known how to defend themselves. In this respect they have demonstrated that they are inferior even to madmen. What could I possibly say that would adequately indicate the tremendous number of stupid things we have done during the last three months? I suffer from a terrible affliction, the worst that can weigh down upon a man endowed with reason: the honor of my country is of much more importance to me than that of my family or of myself. At that rate you can see that whatever road I choose to follow I run the risk of sullying my good name. All this devout *hullabaloo* kicked up by the civil authorities and the gentlemen of the cloth in defense of church properties, people who prefer to save their own skins rather than the life and the honor of their country, has set the final seal on our shame. It has likewise forged the chain of our misfortunes. How could I answer this accusation or explain the rioting which is going on at the very moment when the enemy is landing on the beaches of Veracruz? I confess that I either lack a sufficiently philosophical attitude or that I am too aware of my shame to lift up my head in the presence of the English aristocracy and the assemblies of other nations in the capacity of a representative of the Mexican people, who are looked down upon and scorned by the dregs of Europe. Last night I begged Baranda to withdraw my appointment whose approval is now pending in the Congress, because I am not going to represent Mexico abroad unless some event occurs that will improve our situation. I do not want a victory, nor do I expect one. All I want is the preservation of our honor. I believe that poor General S. A. is suffering as much as I am today, because, brushing aside all polite consideration, he said yesterday that in his profession all the generals, including himself, would hardly make good corporals. He said he wished most ardently that some of the Spanish officers among the Carlist immigrants would apply to him; he would give them jobs. We have realized too late that all of us in our respective professions are no better than corporals! But of course when we judge ourselves we think we are all capable of being generals and admirals! If as a result of our misfortunes we make improvements drawn from the discovery of error, all will not have been lost.

It is not easy to guess just what the end of the war will bring, for, sad to relate, no preparations have been made for anything, not even for peace. In one of his moments of ministerial confusion Rejón threw away the most precious prerogative of the Government by passing on to Congress the resolution regarding the mediation proposed again and again by England. Now, in the terrible division within Congress, the *puro* party has taken the war as its rallying cry with the sole purpose of discrediting and ruining its opponents if they seek to speak peace. And since vanity is our weak point, who knows what monstrous thing a discussion in the Congress may produce, unless a very simple decision is attempted. I believe, however, that peace will come, and very soon, although probably just to cause our old civil strife to flare up again.

Up to the present time we have been living in a continuous state of alarm over the pretensions of Europe's monarchies, fancying, also because of a streak of vanity, that our fate was keeping royal councils from their sleep to quarrel over the rich prize. The last few letters I have received from Paredes bring sad disillusionment, for nothing can make these councils stir a finger to help us against the Americans. They regard our destiny with complete indifference. We shall therefore have to depend entirely upon ourselves.

There is much talk here about the loss of those states.[22] Although their future as Mexicans may not be very agreeable, they can expect nothing as Yankees. Right now they would enter the federation as conquered peoples, and this is all that can be said. The proclamations of McDowell and Harren would be the bases of their future legislation. There is no need to be fooled. The men of the North would not permit themselves to be governed by insignificant little fellows such as usually make up the class of our public officials. These persons are enthusiastic about persecuting people but they are weak when it comes to governing, and they will not be able to serve as models of just and severe impartiality. If the people in those states pursue any other course I am afraid that there will happen to them what Riva Palacio warned us about when the question of a monarchy was being hotly discussed. That is, the genteel educated people will descend to the level of the Indian, and the Indian will descend to the level of the donkey.

I do not know what special events have occurred this morning, for I have spent the entire morning writing this endless letter. I trust you will not be displeased with it, at least as far as *quantity* is concerned. You certainly did not deserve such unlimited obedience, for you have let me go without letters from you for more than a month. Other friends of mine have done the same thing, as if our friendship had gone down in the shipwreck of my job as Minister .

Not even Señor Castañeda has acknowledged receipt of a letter I wrote to him. I have let my pen run on, just as if no one were to read all the scribbling and scratches. Therefore I beg of you to use my revelations carefully. Besides, I do not want you to destroy this letter, because I may need the information in it some time.

Do not return to your old habit of not writing me, even though I myself am not too good a correspondent. The example that I am giving you proves that even if I cannot be depended upon, I pay the arrears with interest at the most unexpected moment. I prize your letters highly for more than one reason, which I shall not enumerate for fear of making you conceited.

Goodbye.

(Signed)

22 Texas, New Mexico, Arizona and California?

CHAPTER V

THE MEXICAN WAR DRAWS TO A CLOSE

Mexico City, April 21, 1847

Señor Don Francisco Elorriaga

My dear friend:

To judge by the long letter I wrote to you, you have probably seen your wishes granted as soon as they were expressed. Honored by the wishes you express in your most recent letter, I shall continue the story that I began, if the disagreeable state of my mind permits me to do so. I shall begin with the latest development.

Our army has been completely routed at Cerro Gordo[1] without any other consolation than that of having preserved its honor. The dispatch which Uraga is to bring in person tonight has not yet been received. But several letters from Jalapa all report the following events. I shall therefore proceed, maintaining my privilege of correcting the details by comparing them with those in the dispatch, if the latter arrives before the special mail is sent out.

Scott attacked our camp with his entire force (15,000 men)[2] forming two columns of 4,000 each, while another of 7,000, making a flanking movement for a distance of about two leagues, got around our lines and attacked S. A. in the rear, setting fire to a dense woods that was on all sides of him. Canalizo, who was in command of the cavalry and some of the infantry in order to cover the rear guard, did little or nothing to stop the enemy. He retreated in complete disorder, leaving our troops caught between two fires. Some say that he did this because he was frightened, and others say it was because he could do nothing else. We do not yet know the facts. S. A. escaped from the midst of the defeated force by cutting through with a column of 400 men under the command of Uraga, who protected him so that he could get away. The letters also state that S. A. then intended to reassemble the scattered troops and that he is now in La Joya with about four or five thousand men. The battle was a very bloody one, and they say it was honorably fought. They agree that the losses total from eight to nine thousand men, including killed and wounded. According to this account we probably lost only 3,000, since S. A. had no more than 8,000 men with him. At the present time 4,000 men ought to be on their way to join him; they had been sent to defend the approaches to the town, but there is nothing to fear in that quarter now. In La Joya some work has already been done on the defenses, and seven cannon are in position there. The guns brought from Perote can be used to increase this number.

1 Town on the highway between Veracruz and Jalapa. The battle lasted about three hours, and on being better informed Ramírez concluded that even honor was lost. See the account in Justin H. Smith, *The War with Mexico* (2 vols., New York, 1919) II, 42-59.

2 Smith states 8,500. Smith, *War with Mexico*, II, 50.

It is five o'clock in the afternoon, and a friend who has just come in from the street says he saw a letter that contradicts the news contained in the others. This letter maintains that our defeat was actually a rout in which our troops scarcely fought at all. There are quite a number of letters disagreeing with this statement, one of them written by Camacho, and this fact should argue for their reliability. I am on pins and needles while waiting for Uraga to get here. He ought to settle our doubts, and I intend to remain at the Ministry until the mail goes out so that I can give you the very latest information. I am going out for a walk and shall leave this letter unfinished, to be completed with news of the happenings. Then this account will be uninterrupted.

Returning to the point where I cut short my previous remarks, I shall give you a brief analysis of the latest developments, because to judge from the confused nature of these and my present distraught state of mind, I shall not be able to include all the details in a single letter.

After the arrival of S. A. the administration worked without rest, moving heaven and earth to concentrate Government action in the manner demanded by the urgency of the situation. But the Congress preferred death rather than to remain in fear of not dying, and furthermore it was dominated by the most scandalous party interests. It obstinately refused to grant the Government extraordinary powers because of its fear that S. A. would instigate a revolt if these were given him.[3] As if on other occasions he needed them to make himself Dictator! The truth of the matter is that the leaders of both factions were afraid that they would lose their political prestige if the Congress gave in. Furthermore each side hoped that it could lay a trap in order to get the better of the other. Out of all this came the idea of having the legislators remove to Celaya, an idea that encouraged the *puros* to hope that they would thus gain a majority of votes, on the supposition that the *moderados,* with their close connections in Mexico City, would not leave their bailiwick. The latter party for this reason resisted the plan of removal, but their resistance was weak. It was finally agreed that Congress would leave when the enemy got to the line of defense at Perote and that thirty deputies were sufficient to carry on deliberations.

The plan was to have been discussed the day before yesterday, but a foolish bit of business came up to exercise a decisive influence on the erratic behavior of the Congress. I mean the plan for a constitution,[4] which Otero has been insisting upon bringing up for the sake of vanished glory. This business has caused serious scandals in the Congress, but in spite of these, he has been insisting on going ahead with the idea in the face of the decree issued yesterday, a copy of which I am sending. Uraga has arrived, and I am out of humor.

3 On April 20 Congress granted the Government power to take all steps necessary to carry on the war, but the Government could not make peace with the United States nor cede any territory to it.
4 This plan was federalistic and in many ways similar to the Constitution of 1824.

Poor Rejón received a terrible scare. Because of a letter that you will find printed in the papers and particularly because of the old hatred against him, he was attacked in his carriage by four *Polkos* and came within an inch of being assassinated. A United States paper attributed it to his connivance with Benton to discuss peace and further stated that Rejón was to share in the 3,000,000.[5] Rejón is said to have taken refuge today in the home of the English Minister.

Uraga has arrived without information, without letters and, I suppose, without even having witnessed the outcome of the battle. To be brief, I suspect that he is a *refugee*. The news he brings merely echoes what we already have heard, and as a result we are still in a horrible state of suspense. The letters from Jalapa do not give news that agrees with his. The important part is that he has no news about S. A. His information is enough to make one burst into tears.

(Signed)

Mexico City, April 25, 1847

Señor Don Francisco Elorriaga

My dear friend:

Things have come to such a pass that we must leave behind us the land of stories and news reports and enter that of serious speculation. But since this time I am going to write *as if I were talking to myself,* I would by no means want my thoughts to suffer the fate of those which Marcus Aurelius consigned to paper, under a similar title—thoughts which today we find translated into all languages. This is a conversation rather than a letter, and in it I propose to tell you whatever comes to my mind just as it occurs. Therefore, I am starting this three days before the mail is due to go out. It will be an immense relief to me, because I cannot speak to anyone else about the subject matter contained in it. I need not say more to you. You may make use of any bit of information that will enable you to pursue your duties as a public official, without including me in the discussions.

Our reverse at Cerro Gordo was a rout as complete as it was shameful. Everything was lost. Absolutely nothing was saved; not even hope, that last consolation the gods left at the bottom of the famous box. A small portion of our troops fought and died heroically; the rest surrendered their arms almost without putting up any defense, or else they ran away. We must consider as lost the soldiers' morale. In them the instincts of race still dominate the fear inspired by the invaders. As for supplies, the less said the better. No money, no muskets, no artillery, not even a fortified

5 President Polk had authorized the sending of Nicholas P. Trist as commissioner to accompany Scott. He was given power to negotiate a treaty with Mexico and could use up to $3,000,000 for this purpose. W. H. Callcott, *Santa Anna* (Norman, Okla., 1936) 262. There is every indication to believe that Santa Anna was to be paid a large sum, around $1,000,000, which would in all probability be used to bribe Mexican congressmen to agree to a treaty ending the war without the necessity of taking Mexico City.

place in which we could take refuge in order to have some point where we could reassemble or effect a retreat. At the time when Canalizo was abandoning the stronghold at Perote,[6] the Government was sending him orders to the same effect, and thus the move was carried out on double authority. Some hours later contrary orders came from General S. A., who intended to make it a base of operations, but there was no longer time to carry out his orders. It is rumored that the Americans are now occupying it. All we have left to compensate us for our misfortunes are the things that have been the sources of all that we deplore: vanity, pride, and lack of cooperation—all in the highest degree. You can judge whether I am mistaken, for I shall give you a brief idea of our fundamental characteristics, as I see them expressed.

Beginning with the men who run our affairs, we find that we have a Congress without prestige, without power and without ability. What is worse, it is undermined and disrupted by partisan hatreds which prevent it from seeing anything clearly, except when it wishes to wound its opponents. You have probably noticed that history records innumerable cases substantiating the oft-repeated saying that "a war with a foreign foe preserves a feeling of nationality and strengthens institutions." In our privileged country quite the contrary has happened on the only two occasions there have been to prove the truth of the maxim: namely, the Spanish conquest under Cortés, and the Yankee conquest under Scott. And to make the terrible comparison complete, both set foot upon the shores of Veracruz during Holy Week. The reason for the difference is clear. A sensible, patriotic people unites and offers a solid front at the first hint of the common peril. A people that is neither sensible nor patriotic grows weak, thus smoothing out difficulties for the invader, who wins without opposition.

But getting back to Congress, I tell you it is a true representative of the people I see around me, because it has evinced a *vocal* enthusiasm for waging war, but a *mental* and even *moral* sluggishness in seeing it through to the finish. I have no doubt that every one of those individuals who on the rostrum or in the public press have so furiously been preaching war to the death, branding as "traitor" anyone who even says one word about a truce, is at heart convinced of our absolute helplessness, not only to carry on the war successfully but even to continue fighting in the face of defeat. Consequently, the end of the conflict is inevitable, whether as the result of a treaty of peace, the result of conquest, or simply because the invader retreats, leaving us what he does not wish to take for himself. I repeat, however, that no one speaks of anything but war; and as the height of contradiction, it is obvious that not one of these advocates of war shows the slightest inclination to shoulder a musket or to put his money into the public treasury. "Let us unite! Let us unite!" some of the friars in the pulpits of Spain were wont to cry. "And *you* go out and fight the French!" That

6 Occupied by the Americans on April 22, 1847.

is what people are shouting here; and since each individual reserves to himself the right to preach, it turns out that we have nothing but preachers. The key to the riddle is simple enough. It is the same with which the public crises of the last ten or twelve years can be explained. The war in Texas was the excuse for the revolutions and corrupt governments of the past. Today this serves as a weapon that each of the quarreling factions wants to get hold of in order to wound its opponents to the death. The first one who talks about peace will lose that weapon, and, therefore, no one wants to utter the fateful word. Another element enters into this question: our national vanity, which, while personifying the nation, will not admit any compromise between victory and complete submission when its pride has been wounded. But it does have a faculty for contenting itself later on with any sort of compromise. These natural inclinations, together with another that is not less characteristic of us—that of putting off doing something until it becomes impossible to put it off any longer—these inclinations, I repeat, have plunged us into a war with regard to which we can say that it has begun, is going on, and will finally drag us on to its conclusion still unprepared.

Although the entire course of our political life could be offered as proof of the foregoing facts, an excellent demonstration can be found in the three latest, very recent events relative to the seizure of church properties, granting of extraordinary powers, and constitutional reforms. In these measures the terrible and the idiotic engage in a fight for supremacy. But yesterday something happened that leaves all these far behind, and I must not go on without mentioning it.

As a consequence of the Cerro Gordo disaster, a motion was made that the Foreign Affairs Committee expedite the matter of mediation proposed by England, a project that has lain dormant since August of last year. Ever since my first days as Minister I made indirect representations as a part of the plan that formed an important element in my political calculations (which you will know about some day). But as I expected, I received no answer and left the matter unsettled, because my chief purpose had already been accomplished. When the project was revived it produced its expected result: a furious storm of insults and accusations with which the *puro* party overwhelmed its opponents. To some extent the latter deserved their fate, because after such a length of time they finally came out with a ridiculous pronouncement. Still, the *puros's* attack was most certainly unjust, because the Committee advised a strictly constitutional procedure. It proposed that the measure be referred to the Government because it was a matter exclusively under Government jurisdiction. If this statement had been made in time, we would not be in our present difficulties, nor would we have to face even more serious ones in store for us. *Although the only point involved was that of the right to proceed with a discussion of the proposal* it occasioned some speeches about "traitors," with serious allusions to the corrupting effect of the $3,000,000 granted by Polk. The storm reached such

proportions that Otero, the originator of the proposal and one of its supporters, voted against it. He did so in spite of the fact that the article
(which had not yet been discussed) had been modified to read that the
Government should act in conformity with the latest law concerning its
powers. For lack of Otero's vote the proposal to discuss the matter was defeated and the question has been deferred until tomorrow. Of course the
whole business was transacted in a session declared to be *strictly secret*.

If we now shift our attention from the Congress, whose character you
already know, to the Government, we find no difference. The latter is only
a reflection of the former as far as inability to get things done is concerned.
Actually Baranda is the only Minister. Although he is resourceful in planning, he lacks the necessary means and assistance to carry out his ideas.
Our good friend, Anaya, is an honest, energetic man who will know how to
die at his post if he remains here, or, as he puts it, *with his gavel in his
hand,* if he has to move elsewhere. His political ideas extend no further than
this, certainly the products of a patriotic heart and a generous soul, but
that is as far as they go. There is a small group of persons, a group that you
probably know, made up of individuals who recognize the really serious
and inevitable nature of our predicament and who also can see a way out.
But although they have all the courage necessary to die, they lack the
strength that it takes to save themselves. They are tinged with the color
that predominates in the Congress. Let us go on to a discussion of finances.

The clergy, desiring to reserve its strength for the final hours, has
demonstrated its munificence, particularly in the matter of religious proces-
sions, although not equally so in church functions, except in preaching. Its
parsimony has been eminently obvious with regard to money, since it has
at last decided to convert its financial aid into a kind of speculation. It is an
occasion for grief and shame to relate what is transpiring. The lack of cash,
the fear that the city will be subjected to bombardment, and the selfishness
of the speculators all have combined to produce a situation in which the
sale of ecclesiastical property has produced no results, although the clergy
itself has solicited purchasers. Thus it is that the promised aid was limited
to a demand that it accept bills of exchange which the Government took
upon itself to negotiate with the brokers. Some church groups refused
to accept these bills, thus showing themselves more Catholic than the
church assembly. The bills of exchange that were accepted have been negotiated at a 40 per cent discount rate. And by whom do you suppose?
By the clergy themselves, with the help of third parties. This will explain
to you the reason why the churches are melting down their silver, a procedure to which the credulity of some newspaper men ascribed such an
honorable motive. The Government has not laid eyes on even one peso
of these promised gifts, and in my presence the order was given to publish
a notice in the press, exposing the real facts regarding them. Several prominent dignitaries of the church have stated that if the Yankees respect
their religion and their property, they can lose nothing through invasion.

This latter point is by no means certain. It would be, however, a circumstance generally desired by all right-thinking men if it meant the *departure* of the invaders afterward. There is no doubt that the attitude of these churchmen is manifesting itself with all the earmarks of atheism, when one recalls the disorders and uprisings against those who formerly defended the liberties of worship. The influence that this apathy or, to be more specific, this lack of faith must have on the outcome of the war is obvious. To appraise clerical influence it is sufficient to recall who had quite contrary feelings in Mexico's war for independence from Spain.

The businessman is not indifferent. On the contrary, although with some misgivings, he is declaring himself to be a confirmed agent of peace. The anger which I am told was caused by Baranda's announcement that he was ordering the removal of cattle, fruit, etc., from the path of the invaders shows quite clearly that we cannot depend upon the unselfishness of the landowners. I am quite sure that they will take advantage of the situation to sell at a good price to any willing buyer and that the Russians during Napoleon's invasion would not have found many to emulate them here. Nor is there a Government sufficiently strict to get things done in spite of resistance.

Help in the form of general contributions, although slow, is productive, certain, and, above all, just. But it has lain dormant upon the mysterious bosom of national sovereignty, which has been concerned only with party quarrels and matters of no relevance to the situation. Thinking only of its daily bread and hoping that our troops would finish off the Yankees and the United States in a single battle, Congress made no preparations for the future. Assuredly this is not a time for requesting general contributions when the enemy is at the very gates of the capital. Of course you will understand that if any demands were made now, nothing would be forthcoming, or, rather, no result could be obtained commensurate with the state of affairs that events have produced.

When a nation gets to such a point of financial distress it does it no good to have a large army or to have a patriotism great enough to build an army if there were means to support it. What happens then when a nation cannot count either upon a large army or upon patriotism? Yet this is precisely the wretched condition we are in. Strictly speaking, the army does not exist. What today bears that name is only a mass of men without training and without weapons. The men assembled at San Luis have disappeared as of by magic, thanks to the scandalous desertions. As far as the guerrillas operating in the eastern part of the country are concerned, you know what they are today. And the scattered remnants of the army now being reassembled by General S. A. cannot, I am sure, do more than delay Scott's onward march, if he does not choose to detach a division of troops to disperse them. He will always have a quicker and less costly way to destroy us by remaining inactive, for we cannot maintain any body of troops much longer. How, then, can we get out of our predicament? You have no doubt seen in the newspapers a notice published with a faith and a degree of enthusiasm beyond all reasonable reflection. The Government has at last put all its hopes in a plan that is supposed to save the country, a plan that has become the central idea of its political maneuvers. This is the one calling for *guerrilla warfare*, the last hope of peoples overwhelmed by superior forces. Recollection of the war in Spain has induced us to take this false step, and we are taking it with the same enthusiasm with which we always take up new and brilliant ideas. The booksellers have experienced a great demand for the history of the Count of Toreno, which has suddenly become a manual of war and freedom. Unfortunately, it has only produced excitement without making any progress as far as our convictions are concerned. The guerrilla bands about which you have probably seen proclamations are not getting many recruits.

But, leaving this matter which cannot but be of vital importance, since without fighters there cannot be a war, the fact remains that the system quite obviously breaks down when one examines the essence of the difficulty with regard to warfare and the general social system. Spain, and other peoples who found themselves in a like situation, owed the successful outcome of their efforts to a conjunction of various circumstances that are not the same here. The principal ones could be listed as follows: first, they were struggling against a war of *conquest;* second, they were waging their battle in a small, well-populated territory where people could quickly assemble for mutual protection, with the added circumstance of a profound interest in the preservation of their soil because of the manner in which their territory was distributed; third, these same circumstances, added to a robust national spirit, which was manifested by a hatred of the foreigner, impelled them to pursue the invaders. Even the individual was considered an enemy, because he was not considered indispensable to the prosperity of the nation. To sum up: the spirit of political unity represented by the monarchy or by a government that was in harmony with the country and a spirit of social unity injected into the very veins of the people by the instinctive conviction that union gives advantages, were the organizing factors of those various circumstances. By working together, these elements gave success to the unselfish efforts of a people that had been unjustly brought under a foreign yoke. The banner of war remains standing as long as the chief of state lives, no matter where he happens to be. When he succumbs, then he is replaced by the national spirit, which preserves the unity of a people. Think a little about our situation and you will perceive that none of those influences I have mentioned can have any effect on us, and that even if we could rely upon almost all the influences that we need, the lack of two of them which can clearly be noted, would suffice to render all the rest useless. The war that we are waging is not one of conquest, but of dismemberment. Nor do we have even a shred of unity. On the contrary, the fact that some of our territory will be wrested from us is a question assuming such proportions that it is actually being looked upon as a means of liberation.

Note: (I shall not send this letter, because I do not wish to give an erroneous impression or inspire a lack of confidence in the situation. I shall continue it as a *memorandum* concerning the most recent developments.)

Although today, the 25th, is a holiday, the Congress was to convene to consider the question of mediation. But there was no session owing to the lack of a quorum.

26

After the second reading the proposal was brought up for discussion, and, when it came time for the vote, there was no quorum because two *puros* had left. One of these was Navarro, who had fought the measure with the greatest bitterness.

The famous committee which produced the *first plan to maintain the war against the Americans* was called into session the same day. The plan itself was an everlasting monument of ineptitude and confusion and was printed on large sheets of paper posted on street corners. I have a copy among my documents. It caused more alarm than the invasion by the Americans because it quite illegally called upon the brokers and the monarchists for the purpose of compelling them to defray the expenses of the war, while it refrained from censuring the landowners, the ruined business-men, and the common people. This clearly illustrates its tendencies. The proposed plan of defense provides for the arming of 50,000 men with lances, daggers, and machetes in order to carry on the guerrilla warfare that will devastate the country, even without the fighting against the foreigner. Furthermore, the document is characteristic of the times.

27

There was no meeting of Congress because of the lack of a quorum. This time it was the *moderados* who left because they feared possible reinforcements brought in by their opponents. It must be explained that the failure of a sufficient number of members to appear applies to the secret session at which the question of mediation was to be taken up, and does not apply to the public session where they calmly went on discussing the perennial question about the constitution. This will be a double calamity for the country.

28

Although Baranda had previously shown enthusiasm for the war, he finally lost hope and worked actively, though secretly, for mediation as the only way to save the capital from invasion by the Americans. Another piece of business fraught with grave consequences for both the Government and the cause of the people was to have been taken up today; namely, the reinstatement of the Oaxaca officials who had been driven out of office by an uprising. The Government was against the measure because the present officials have aided the national cause by providing many troops and large sums of money, whereas the deposed officials had not done so, thereby incurring public disfavor throughout the state. It was not possible, however, to put the former authorities back into office without resorting to armed force, which the Government did not have. And it could not have done so without running the risk of depriving itself of needed assistance. With this in mind, the Government entered into talks with several deputies to get them to attend the session while the question of mediation was being discussed, after which they were to leave the Chamber so as to prevent a vote on the Oaxaca affair. But the plan went even further than this; it contemplated continued lack of a sufficient number of members so that by this indirect means the Congress would be destroyed, since it had become an insuperable obstacle to the progress of public affairs. But just the reverse occurred, because the Oaxaca measure was put through, the deposed authorities being reinstated. Nothing was done about the matter of mediation, which was tabled for the following session. How can such an event be explained? Quite easily and in a way which illustrates the pattern of our affairs and the standards of our public men. Otero insisted that his plan for a reform of the constitution be carried out immediately, because in his pitiful vanity he wanted to appear as his country's reformer. In order to carry out his purpose he made an agreement with the Oaxaca delegation, promising to vote favorably on the measure referred to above and to urge his party to vote for it, provided the Oaxaca delegates voted for his plan for reform.

Baranda considered mediation not only as a means of ending the war but also as an indirect way to prolong it with fewer disadvantages in the event that peace could not be secured, although in the latter case he expressed ideas that were to a certain extent incompatible. He has been getting secret aid from the English residents of the city and particularly from an Irish priest, who for some time has been planning a colonization project in California, in my opinion as a secret agent of England. Relying upon such aid, Baranda conceived the plan of getting the Irishmen in Scott's forces to desert so as to enlist them in our army, offering them as inducements ten pesos, payment for their muskets and, in addition, two hundred acres of land at the end of the war. Two agents were needed for this transaction, one in charge of distributing the announcements in the American army, together with plans, etc., while the other was to inform General S. A. of the matter and attend to the guarantees that were to be offered the Irish. Payno, *Don Simplicio's* editor, was given the first assignment, and it was proposed that I be given the second.

I had three serious objections to the plan. The first was that S. A. might misunderstand the situation and think that the Government and I had decided that he ought to discuss peace terms, in which event I would get the worst of it. The second difficulty was that S. A. might not fully comply with the agreement made with the deserters because of his uneconomical, inefficient management of funds. In the third place, I was afraid that the plan for desertion might become an insurmountable obstacle to the peace that was desired and also an excuse to make the war a bloody one. As to the first difficulty, it was decided that under some good pretext I was to get a letter from S. A. to Pedraza, which the General was to write him concerning a peace settlement, thus showing that he was in complete sympathy with the project. The second objection was removed by the decision not to entrust to S. A. the money (60,000 pesos) with which to pay the deserters. Instead he was authorized to draw payment against certain tax resources. The third difficulty I believed to be incapable of solution, because once preliminary peace discussions were begun, Scott would not allow his army to be corrupted nor would he look on calmly while it was disintegrating in order to swell the ranks of his foes. Since I did not believe that this would be the way to terminate the matter once and for all, I stated my convictions explicitly to Baranda, confining my remarks entirely to only two extreme points, since I saw no middle way: either we should come out openly for peace or go on with the war until we were completely overwhelmed by the U. S. In the latter case we could force them either to retreat or to crush us. Each of these extremes had its peculiar advantages and disadvantages. The first was more favorable to our national honor, but it would imply a terrible situation for our country because of the disorder and reversion to old evils that peace would bring. The second would help to increase the population by providing the country from time to time with large numbers of colonists; on the other hand this would react to the detriment of the present generation and of our race in forcing us to go through the miseries of the conquest. Baranda wanted me to leave on the third day, but I did not want to do this until Congress had done something about the mediation question.

During the last several days the numbers of our officers and other officials coming in as refugees from the battle of Cerro Gordo have been increasing scandalously. One General [Rangel] and seven officers were held up by three bandits, who paid them the insulting compliment of returning their swords. All these officers were eloquent examples of discouragement, terror, and a desire for peace.

29

A proposal to discuss the mediation was voted upon in Congress and was given preliminary approval by a vote of thirty-six to thirty-five. The business could have been considered as definitely settled because the measure contained only one article, but efforts were made to drag it into a special discussion. There were more than enough members present to make this move successful.

This morning Baranda again urged me, as he did last night, to leave tomorrow for a conference with General S. A. But I finally made him understand that the Government, and especially I myself, would be terribly compromised if the Congress were to vote down the mediation measure and that as long as this matter was not definitely settled the success of my mission would be quite uncertain.

30

The mediation proposal was rejected and sent back to the committee. Therefore I did not want to have my conference with General S. A. Baranda thought seriously of resigning his post in the Ministry, and I even drew up the draft of his resignation, the reasons being the disagreement in the Cabinet and the confusion with which measures were drawn up. Each Minister was acting on his own.

May 1

The lack of agreement on the part of the Cabinet as a whole, in spite of the harmony that existed among the individual members themselves, coupled with the question as to whether the Congress ought to remain in continuous session, posed two insurmountable obstacles, not only to waging war but also to negotiating peace. Baranda did not want to continue in his office as Minister unless both these problems could be solved immediately. Rodríguez Puebla, Pedraza, and Riva Palacio, who were in complete accord with Baranda on the matter, took it upon themselves to clear up the situation. They therefore had a conference with Otero to get him to bring about a recess of the Congress and to arrange the dismissal of the ministers with President Anaya. Baranda insisted that Pedraza be given the post of Minister of War, and Rosa that of Justice, in order to please the people of Zacatecas. I cannot recall who was suggested for the post of Finance Minister. Anaya was in a mood to accept mediation despite the compromises in which he had placed himself by his sudden proclamation. Otero behaved like a hypocrite, maneuvering in all imaginable ways and even resolutely declaring that the Congress would continue in session. All this got him into trouble with his old friends. The secret of his behavior lay in the fact that he wanted to receive sanction for his constitutional reform program, the principal idea of which was to make him the law-giver for Mexico; he was sacrificing everything for this puerile goal. Revealing first one aspect of his character and then another, he stated that as a newspaper man he strongly supported the prosecution of the war. As a deputy he played the part of a sad, quiet politician. However, he secretly went to Baranda to force him to accept mediation, totally ignoring the Congress, and promised to help support him. I have a suspicion that he intends to play a clever trick on Baranda so as to profit by the latter's defeat. He hates Baranda, just as he hates any man of recognized merit. No trouble was experienced as far as the President was concerned.

At this time MacIntosh[7] arrived with a request from the English Minister[8] to prevent Baranda's resignation, asking him to defer any such deci-

7   Spelled *Mackintoch* in the text. He was the British consul in Mexico City.
8   Charles Bankhead.

sion until May 3 and assuring him that effective steps had been taken to secure a majority in the Congress, thus practically assuring the successful passage of the measure. Meanwhile, the Cabinet members discussed the feasibility of putting an end to that embarrassing organization by indirect means whereby some of the deputies were to be induced to leave in order that there might not be the requisite number. Bribes were freely passed around, but the victory was only temporary. The only result was that there were no sessions either that day or during the days immediately following, until the 7th, the only exception being one held on the 3rd, which was of no importance.

7

This lengthy interval encouraged the Cabinet members to hope that Congress would not convene again, and during this time events of great importance to the future of the country transpired. The passage of the constitutional reform bill was being held up by *only one* article, and Otero found himself in imminent danger of being shipwrecked, as it were, just before reaching shore. This development drove him nearly frantic, impelling him to continue his efforts and sacrifice everything for the sake of his program. Yesterday the Government had sent back[9] . . . the decree that ordered the reinstatement of the Oaxaca authorities. Thereupon the Oaxaca delegation protested, saying that they would not attend the sessions and made hasty preparations to return home. If they had done so, the Congress would have irrevocably come to an end. In the midst of this anxious situation Otero approached the Oaxacans and promised to see that harmony was re-established in Congress if they would only attend and vote for his bill. This they consented to do, demanding only that the Oaxaca question be taken up first under suspension of the rules. Otero was opposed because he wanted his constitutional reform bill to be voted on first. He was afraid that if the Oaxaca issue were lost the deputies might leave immediately thereafter and there would not be a sufficient number of them left to vote on his measure. The Oaxacans, on the other hand, feared that if the pending article were passed, Otero would then have no interest in pushing their measure through. Finally they reached an agreement, wherein their matter of business would be handled as if it were a simple resolution. To carry out the plan, the Government's reservations on the Oaxaca decree were considered in secret session. It was requested that next the reservations be discussed by the committee and that the Committee retire to present its report later during the same session, the public session continuing meanwhile to discuss the constitution bill. About four o'clock in the afternoon the Committee reported *unfavorably*, and although a demand was made for the suspension of other business it was not granted, and the Oaxaca matter was postponed until the following day as the first order of business.

9 Here the text is corrupt: "El Gobierno había devuelto, ayer . . . rvaciones el decreto que, etc."

There were many added proposals relative to the constitutional reform bill pending in committee, but since Otero was apprehensive lest the bird escape from his hand and since there was some disagreement among the Committee members, he overcame all difficulties, in the absence of any report on the bill, by presenting another that he called "a special vote." He then proposed that all the added suggestions and plans be left for the new Congress to consider and that the present Congress limit itself to approving the bill under consideration. This was as much as to say: "Only my bill should pass, and I ought to be the one and only legislator." As was to be expected, he offended and antagonized several of the deputies. The question remained unsettled.

Deputy Alcalde, a *puro* in sympathies and a candidate for office, proposed that Congress annul all the decrees of the Government issued by virtue of the extraordinary powers granted it. This clearly indicated that on the political scene one authority or the other was superfluous: either the Congress or the Government, and that in the course of time one would inevitably absorb the other, or else both would disappear under the sword of the invader.

In the meantime another event of the greatest significance occurred. The English Minister, now convinced that absolutely nothing could be expected from the Congress in the matter of clearing the way for mediation, offered to make peace proposals himself or, rather, to act as Scott's emissary for any that he might make. In this way all the more serious difficulties associated with the parleys would be avoided. He furthermore promised that the American army would not advance, and thus some agreement could be arrived at. It was hoped that the Congress would be pacified by such a step, when it saw England's sword flung in the balance. The following measures were adopted.

8

The report of the Committee relative to reinstating the Oaxaca authorities was approved. This was tantamount to making certain that either the Government would be embarrassed by this act of disobedience or that the number of troops facing the enemy would be diminished for the purpose of sending some of them against the people of Oaxaca, who would thus be repaid by civil war for the good services they had rendered the cause of the nation. It was all the more terrible since Santa Anna's principal force consisted of troops from Oaxaca under the command of General León, who had been instrumental in bringing about a change in the officials.[10] Although the Government in its opposition was defending quite noble principles, it had a secret interest known only to Baranda, who was protecting it. On the 15th there was to be held the election for the President of the Republic, and since there was no assurance that this office would devolve upon S. A., it was a question of making certain that the power which he had ob-

10 In Oaxaca.

tained provisionally would continue. Thus it would be necessary to prevent a legal election from being held; in other words, three-fourths of the legislatures must be kept from voting. In this way dictatorial power would be assured him, or at least he would be assured of powers almost as great, because if the Congress could be abolished—the absence of eight or ten deputies would assure this result—the Government would stand alone to face the situation, and the Government had already been granted extraordinary powers. The Oaxaca affair, therefore, was one of the greatest importance, since if the former officials were not reinstated there would be no legislature in the state, and without a legislature no presidential election could be held. Several other states were in the same predicament.

During the night an anonymous request was sent to the Vice-governor of Oaxaca urging him not to permit the deputies to meet and to disperse them if necessary, so that they could not hold election proceedings.

Onslaughts against the Government are continuing in Congress. Deputy Alcalde brought accusations against the Minister of War because of the order restricting the freedom of the press. I wonder what these men understand by the expression "extraordinary powers" and how they relate them to responsibility.

The greatest discouragement is noted in Puebla where the Governor, in a confidential letter to Baranda, declares that the city is absolutely without any means of defense and cannot even depend upon public sentiment to resist the Americans. The Prefect issued a proclamation dealing with the Yankee invasion. It may be considered a literal copy of the one issued by Taylor in Saltillo.

The Congress continues with its discussions about the constitution without even a glance at the country's plight as to whether to go on with the war or sue for peace.

The uncertainty that Baranda has experienced the last few days with regard to remaining in the Ministry is beginning to disappear. Although, in my opinion, he feels a secret aversion to giving up his portfolio, he has convinced himself that a propitious moment for resigning with honor has arrived, unless he decides to keep his post with all its attendant problems. For several days now Rodríguez Puebla, Pedraza, and Riva Palacio have been discussing plans with the President relative to changes in the Cabinet and the suspension of the Congress as indispensable means of getting the situation under control, with the understanding that the Cabinet be reorganized as Baranda sees fit. Those suggesting this plan have worked so slowly and the President has manifested such a lukewarm attitude that there is reason to believe they have a secret plan, part of which involves the dismissal of Baranda. Perhaps they wish to get him out of the Cabinet because they intend to overthrow S. A. and they wish to spare the Minister, since he has rendered them very important service. The following episode would seem to confirm this supposition.

MacIntosh[11] had a conference with Baranda with a view toward getting him to retire from office. Baranda tells me that when he opposed this suggestion he [MacIntosh][12] proposed that he resign at an opportune moment, but working in agreement with the President so that it might be made the occasion for the dismissal of the other ministers, it being understood that Baranda would be recalled to his old post when the Ministry was reorganized. Although he was resigning against his will, Baranda agreed to the plan and requested Riva Palacio to have a talk with the President about the matter by way of putting the plan into effect. But Riva excused himself, advising Baranda not to depend entirely upon the President's promises even if given with complete assurance, because Otero and other friends might make him change his mind. This reply and the eager efforts made by Rodríguez and even Riva himself to get Baranda to give up his portfolio immediately caused people to suspect that they were in on the secret plan and that at any cost they wanted to get rid of him. I, too, suspected as much and frankly told him so. I urged him to resign in view of the fact that his efforts to stay in office would be futile and that by staying he might get involved in the storm. There was reason to fear that Otero might engage in some intrigue with this thought in mind and that he might be trying to secure a post in the Ministry in order to get his constitutional reform bill put through. He had told several deputies that the ministers were doing such a bad job that he felt "tempted to ask Anaya to appoint him to the Ministry." This arrogant attitude may have been the result of one of his frequent exhibitions of childish vanity. But everything must be feared in the case of an ambitious man of no particular importance and without a trace of modesty.

10

Baranda has resigned, giving as his reasons the lack of cooperation among the ministers and the issuing of the Oaxaca decree. The Council of Ministers had been in session since half-past eight, and Baranda did not appear, although he was repeatedly summoned. At eleven o'clock at night he handed his resignation to the President. The latter acted as if he were going to refuse it and even went so far as to declare that he would not open the envelope containing it. But perhaps this was only a demonstration of gallantry.

11

This morning a special dispatch arrived advising us of S. A.'s march to Puebla and Scott's advance in the same direction. Government spies and private communications bring us news that depresses us and makes us feel the shame of it all. Here is the gist of it.

The Yankees have at their disposal some 7,000 men and an immense artillery train for their military operations. They have 2,000,000 pesos in

11   *Makintosch* in the text.
12   Inserted by editor.

their coffers and pay cash for their subsistence and transport, threatening dire punishment for anyone who refuses to sell his produce to them. In contrast with this situation is the one our troops are facing. They have nothing and use force in obtaining what they need, either paying nothing at all or paying grudgingly.

Groups of soldiers like those of Cortés inflict terrible punishment for the death of any Yankee. The mayor of a town is made responsible, and his own private property is confiscated if it can be proved that such an act occurred with his knowledge. Our guerrilla troops have been denied the benefits of human rights and have been declared highwaymen. Their accomplishments, however, do not give cause for high hopes. They take up their positions in the woods and after firing their muskets they run away. Up to now they have been able to seize only one wagon.

The wounded in Jalapa are suffering the greatest privations and misery. Impelled by the urgency of the situation, they leave the hospitals and perish in the open country, where the ground is strewn with corpses and cast-off war equipment. Putrefaction has set in.

In Jalapa the Yankees were received in a friendly manner, and the Prefect made a present of a bouquet of flowers to Scott. It is said that dances have been given in Scott's honor.

The families that had fled from Puebla because of fear of the enemy returned to the city, but left it in throngs as soon as they heard that S. A. was approaching. "You cannot find even one donkey to ride on," they have been telling Don Antonio Haro.[13] Families leave on foot, and terror is reflected on everyone's face. General S. A.'s enemies attribute this exodus to the hatred professed for him and to the fear inspired by the excesses he is said to have committed in Orizaba[14] and which were carried out in order to obtain supplies. But the truth is that the people of Puebla are afraid that he may try to resist Scott and that this will force them to defend themselves. The people had resigned themselves to the situation and were determined to bear their yoke. That is why the Prefect anticipated their desires by issuing the orders he thought would please them.

S. A.'s division consisting of about 4,500 men is in a serious condition, especially in the case of the cavalry. Álvarez was coming to their support with 3,000 men, but these troops cannot be relied upon because they know how to carry on only a guerrilla warfare and this only in their own districts. General Rangel, who ran away at the battle of Cerro Gordo, deserting his command when the action had scarcely begun, has merited the confidence of the Government, which has sent him to Puebla with some artillery and money to help S. A. Under a system like this it is impossible not only to carry on a war but also to secure peace and any kind of order.

During the last eight or ten days Valencia has continued to request that

13 The Governor.
14 City between Veracruz and Puebla.

he be put in command of some troops, and he has been alternately encouraged and deceived by offers of a command in the contingents from San Luis or Puebla. But since no command has been forthcoming he has indicated his extreme displeasure, and it will not be surprising if he instigates a revolt, should the opportunity present itself. He wanted a respectable reserve force to be organized with himself at the head in order, as he expressed it, "that a decent peace may be obtained in the event that necessity forces us to accept it." His intention was obvious. If such a thing can be done with the troops that the states of the interior intend to place under arms *to defend themselves against the national Government,* the command will be entrusted to Bustamante.

S. A. writes very angrily about Bravo's appointment as chief commander in Mexico City. S. A. certainly does not understand his true situation, since he believes that he still enjoys his former popularity and prestige. He cannot even count upon his old help, the army, because the cowardly officers and leaders who fled from the enemy are united in blaming him for their misfortune. Some of them attribute it to his lack of skill, and others to his conniving with the enemy. This last accusation has been spread around through the troops in order to discourage them, and the Yankees themselves have assured their prisoners that it is true. The intrigue and its purpose are well known.

The troops have come back very much depressed. The leaders and officers declare that the Yankees are *invincible,* and the soldiers are telling terrible tales that bring to mind the Conquest. Some say that the enemy soldiers are such huge, strong men that they can cut an opponent in two with a single sweep of their swords. It is also said that their horses are gigantic and very fast and that their muskets discharge shots which, once they leave the gun, divide into fifty pieces, each one fatal and well-aimed. Let us say nothing about their artillery, which has inspired fear and terror in all our troops and is undeniable proof of our backwardness in military art.

The question of the war has assumed a frightening aspect. If we go on fighting we shall surely be conquered, and if we sue for peace we cannot expect any good from the people of the interior of the country from whence come the destructive elements that are gnawing at the vitals of the nation. What are we going to do with the numerous, filthy remnants of the army? What shall we do with this host of leaders and officers? And what shall we do about the anarchy and disorder now enthroned and masked beneath the mantle of the federation? The states are now in a position to disregard orders without fear of reprisals, and they are making a great ado about it. Even a fifteen-year-old girl is not as precise in matters of honor as those states are in respect to their inflated sovereignty. The ultra-democratic party[15] is proclaiming that the war is one way that should lead us to con-

15 The *puros.*

quest, fancying that in this manner we can go on to obtain perfect freedom. This is their program.

In order to spare himself any compromising situations, Baranda decided to spend the day on his estate in San Angel, and I accompanied him. Upon our return in the evening we learned that the President had sent for him several times and that it was rumored we had gone to Puebla to come to an understanding with General S. A.

The newspaper known as the *Razonador,* whose policy is to defend the advantages of a peace settlement, came out with an announcement today. In the public press I am being mentioned as one of the editors of this paper, just as I was said to have been the editor of *El Tiempo.* But up to the present time I have had no part in it. Three or four days ago Baranda suggested that I do some writing for *Razonador,* making a big mystery of who its contributors were. The rumor is that they are people of consequence.

12

The President has not yet opened the envelope containing Baranda's resignation and keeps on calling upon him *with the hope that Baranda may respond.* The President went to see Rodríguez, Pedraza, and Riva to ask for some explanation, since there was no doubt that they were keeping secret their plan, which involved Baranda. We supposed that their efforts to get him out of the Ministry were simply the result of their friendship and the present situation, since if Baranda accepted the Ministry post he did so because of their insistence and he would rightly expect them not to desert him in the midst of the trouble. Now we have discovered that they have been proceeding without any plan or agreement and that their sole purpose was to facilitate or, rather, compel Baranda's resignation because of the ominous aspect that the situation presented. Their assistance was not required in this matter, for Baranda had a short conference with the President, whose chief purpose was to arrange for a meeting with several individuals for tomorrow, and Baranda reserved the right to explain during this meeting the conditions under which he might consider resuming his post.

13

Baranda insisted that Rodríguez, Pedraza, Riva, and Otero attend this meeting with the President and there presented his conditions. They involved the immediate dismissal of the Ministers of Justice and War [Suárez Iriarte and Gutiérrez] and a demand that on the day after tomorrow the Congress should be declared in recess and the *moderado* party be required to cooperate in the reorganization of the Cabinet. Otero had been chosen to attend to these matters, but he has upset everything and created difficulties in his double capacity of deputy and journalist. He immediately showed a hostile attitude because discussion of his constitutional reform bill had not yet been completed. He did, however, promise the Government help from his party in Congress. Riva and Rodríguez resolutely opposed him and openly indicated their mistrust of the certainty and effectiveness of his promises, maintaining that as long as the Congress continued in session it constituted an obstacle to any free action by the Government. Baranda took advantage of this opportunity to urge Otero to take a post in the Ministry and assume the risk, since he had so much confidence in his influence over Congress. The others talked to him in a similar vein. But he refused to go so far as to assume such a responsibility. He could see that everyone was blaming him as the real author of the difficulties that beset the Government and of the obstacles that had been put in its path, and he declared that he would act otherwise and on different principles if the Congress would approve his reform bill. If it would, then he would see to it that an adjournment was declared for the day after tomorrow and that the *Republicano* would espouse the Government's cause.

The Cabinet change was then made with Baranda's approval. He designated Don Luis de la Rosa for the post of Minister of Justice and General Alcorta for that of War. Orders were immediately sent out to Suárez Iriarte and Gutiérrez to submit their resignations. When these matters had been attended to, the President handed Baranda's letter of resignation back to him, but the latter refused to accept it and stated that his resignation would continue in force as long as he was not given a guarantee that the agreement would be carried out. He furthermore stated that he would again assume his duties if the Congress were adjourned the day after tomorrow; otherwise he would remain out of the Cabinet. To effect this adjournment it was necessary that only a few deputies retire, and it was quite possible that Otero might not want to be among them, because he wished to maintain his popularity and not show an indifferent attitude toward the basic principles he had defended in the *Republicano* so as to keep the other deputies in line. Riva Palacio told Otero that they both should be the first to set an example by not attending the sessions, and it was so agreed. But I am afraid that Otero may play a trick on everybody concerned.

A special dispatch from the Governor of Puebla arrived at noon. It tells of the announcement issued on the 12th by Worth, second in command of the Americans, to the effect that the city would be occupied on the 15th. As a consequence Worth suggests that a commission be sent to him to discuss ways and means of assuring public order and the safety of the citizens and their possessions. Worth threatens to bombard the city if the Governor does not comply. The city had been almost deserted anyway, because no one wished to defend it, nor even thought of doing so. The Governor does not add one word of hope or comfort and limits himself to copying Worth's note and informing the Government that he has also communicated the contents to S. A. According to rumor, the latter is said to have planned to evacuate the city immediately and retire to San Martín Tezmelucán.

Baranda has returned to his post in the Cabinet full of hope and enthusiasm and is displaying the greatest activity. He has adopted and immediately put into effect a plan of Valencia's and has arranged for the latter to march out with a division of 4,000 men and twelve pieces of artillery, taking a short cut so as to take up a position between Puebla and Tepeyahualco and cut off Worth, thereby leaving him in camp in Puebla. Every effort will be made to prevent him from getting food and supplies, since it is known that he has only six days' rations on hand. I think we are engaging in a desperate gamble and that if the affair turns out badly for us it will be the last attack we can make—perhaps the most humiliating of all our reverses. If these operations result in giving us more time, more than 12,000 men can be mobilized against Worth. So much the worse for us if he defeats this force. Baranda made arrangements today for the departure of Valencia's division and all its supplies, and although it was said that the division will leave tomorrow, it is probable that it will not be until Monday. Who knows whether in the meantime the enemy will not attempt an attack against S. A. and thereby with a single blow destroy our plans and our hopes?

Fear is increasing here in proportion as the enemy gets nearer, and it is not a remote possibility that a revolution will break out against anyone who tries to defend himself if the enemy gets to the city. During the last few days there has been some talk about a couple of insurrectionist movements, and the Government is showing some alarm. It has been said that Bravo wanted to start an uprising on behalf of the Constitution of 1843 and the re-convening of the Congress of 1846. Valencia was credited with wanting to bring about the same thing through a dictatorship, with himself as Dictator.

The *puros* and the *moderados* in the Congress effected a plan *to save the nation* by means of commissioners named for the purpose. The plan consisted of *adding two more articles* to the new constitutional amendment!

(Signed)

Mexico City, May 8, 1847

My dear friend:

It was with a feeling of sincere and profound regret that I learned your long silence was caused by an illness I had not known about. Since I did not know how to explain this silence of yours, I was naturally quite vexed. Viewed in another light, the news was timely, because to tell you the truth I did not know how to write to you. The proof of this is that after I had started a letter to you, which took up three pages with its introduction, I left it unfinished because I did not have the heart to send it. In all this I was influenced by the scornful silence the new Governor has maintained with respect to me, a silence for which I never cease thanking God, since you who supported him and were so happy over his election must have shown my letter to him, in spite of my request to the contrary. It did not please me at all. The mistake cannot be rectified now. One moment has sufficed to destroy the work of years and countless efforts. We have descended to our natural level, and every day I am exposed to the mortification of epigrams justly directed at me. To excite you further I shall tell you that people in Durango have been writing letters to this city, assuring me that all of this was your work and was well planned. I suspect that it was one of those mistakes you are in the habit of making when too much confidence has been placed in you. But let us proceed to other matters and not bother any more about what cannot be helped.

Our situation is truly desperate. Everything, absolutely everything, is lost, and judging by the way things are going it is doubtful whether we can save our independence, the last refuge and symbol of our honor. The animosity and indolence of the political parties that have been quarreling over the possession of power have left us only two ways of escape: either conquest or a peace settlement that will always be a shameful one, because we do not have the strength to reject any peace terms that may be offered us. The second way has been rejected, and do not think that it has been because of bravery, but because of vanity and cowardice on the part of some persons, perhaps also because of—treason, for the thirst for vengeance and no doubt an exaggerated patriotism are clothed in other garb so as not to frighten us with their ugliness. Since the continuation of the war in the expectation of signal success is an impossibility it will inevitably result in our being completely overwhelmed; and since *effective* resistance is bound to grow less day by day, the ease with which the Americans are winning must inspire them with the idea of conquest, which they undoubtedly will be able to realize. With matters brought to this stage, we shall be reduced to the status of *colonies,* and the rosy dreams of some enthusiasts who are raving about the quick regeneration of the independent states will be shattered by the clanking of their irksome chains.

Although the peace party is very large, especially among the equally large and unspeakable remnants of our broken army, no one is brave enough to propose peace; but they assuredly are brave enough to let themselves be conquered without a struggle. These persons are not demanding peace, but they do become alarmed at every attempt made by the Government to put up a defense, and this populous city can hardly wait to drive the Government out, fearing it more than the plague. Yesterday I received two disillusioning blows that have overwhelmed me. The Governor of Puebla has sent a *very confidential* message to the Minister of Foreign Affairs in which he states that he cannot be at all certain that the city will offer the least resistance to the enemy and that the greatest despondency is noted throughout the entire state, since it played a large part in the disaster at Cerro Gordo. Rangel had a conference with the President and advised him that the troops were refusing to march *because the Yankees were in overwhelming numbers!* For some time now Olaguível has been declaring himself in open opposition to the Government and has been taking pride in refusing to obey it. His example has been contagious, and other governors are doing the same thing. Only one state, Oaxaca, has stood firm, true and even heroic, providing all it can in troops and money in the midst of its suffering. But Congress, that accursed institution, the perennial source of evil and the obstacle to everything that is good, has bent its efforts toward destroying even that small element of resistance. The history of the Congress is sad and shameful.

You know that a revolution in Oaxaca drove out the authorities, who were extreme *puros* and also extremely useless. The Oaxaca deputies in the Congress proposed a measure declaring the new government null and void, which the national Government stubbornly resisted for two powerful reasons. The first was that it was necessary to make the restoration by force of arms, and the Government had no available weapons. The other reason was that the Government would otherwise be deprived of numerous useful sources of help which the state is at present providing it. In spite of this the nullification measure was passed, and although the Government sent it back to the Congress with appended remarks indicating that there were no facilities for carrying it out, Congress at the present time, by dispensing with the business on hand, has been discussing the possibility of bringing the measure up again in order to start civil strife in that state. You will be right in asking, "Why all this effort?" I do not like to say it, nor would I tell anyone but you. Otero thought he would assume the immortal aureole by posing as the restorer of his country's constitution and has sacrificed everything to his puerile vanity, including his own country. During his struggle with an institution that has been falling to pieces he has spared no effort to keep it going so that he could get his constitutional amendment passed. The Oaxaca deputation escaped from his clutches, and he offered to help their cause if they would only remain. He has rendered this assistance. The influence of Rodríguez, Pedraza, and Riva Palacio has failed to convince him, and he has preferred to come into open conflict with them rather than give up his mania. Yesterday his hopes and the sacrifices he has made seemed to be on the verge of disappointment, for the Oaxacans had walked out of Congress. But a new agreement was made in which their business was to be considered first, and thus a full list of deputies was secured. The sinister results of all this were immediately realized, since here was a deputy who had proposed that the decrees granting the Government extraordinary powers be revoked. Perhaps you already have imagined what course we are set for and the fate that lies in store for us.

While such idiotic things are going on in preparation for still more idiotic ones, the cardinal issue, that of life or death, remains in the hands of the committee on the reform of the constitution. The committee has said nothing nor does it want to say anything about mediation by England, either to accept or to reject it in plain terms. It is also to be noted that on the very day the *Republicano* declared itself opposed to the measure the author of the article approached Baranda to advise him to accept mediation without considering the Congress in the matter. What hopes can you derive from such politics? The report that was submitted ten or twelve days ago proposing that the mediation measure be returned to the Government so that it might exercise its constitutional prerogatives, under the limitations imposed by the decree granting extraordinary powers, was approved in the General Assembly by the margin of one vote. Although the article of amendment should have been carried also, it was rejected the following day by more than twenty votes without any reasons being given for such action. It was sent back to the committee where it still remains. These developments have given rise to the contention that the constitutional powers of the Government have been restricted. Although this may be an absurd charge, it is certain that as long as Congress is in session the Government will not exercise its prerogatives because it is timid about undelegated authority. *Just between you and me,* the whole Cabinet, including the President, is convinced of the Government's helplessness; it wants to accept mediation but does not dare to do so because it fears Congress, *which holds the same convictions.* Both groups are afraid of those who shout for war.

The latter group is composed of two kinds of persons, utterly heterogeneous in complexion, and I am almost persuaded to join one of these elements. In order to know them well, one would have to classify them according to the principle that determines their convictions. One side believes or affects to believe, out of vanity, selfishness or patriotism, that in the long run we can win the struggle, expelling the enemy from all our territory. Or else if such a thing cannot be done we can at least go down fighting with our honor intact, following the example set at Numancia. Among this group one finds banded together the youthful enthusiasts who rely only on their optimism and who, having nothing to lose, see some hope of gain. In this group is also a crowd of *guerrillas,* who, by carrying on a warfare based on expediency and profit to themselves, intend to live off the country, seizing upon the little left by the enemy to complete the picture of desolation. Then there are all those other individuals, who, out of vanity or a sense of patriotism, think it would be infamous to conclude a peace with a wicked enemy whose only right was that of superior numbers and equipment, even though this superiority has been belittled and scorned because of our very vanity itself and the enemy has been branded with the epithet of "a handful of cowardly adventurers." So much the worse for us!

The other faction is made up of two kinds of individuals, also dissimilar, but who have at least something in common in so far as they believe that the war cannot go on and that our defeat is inevitable. Part of this faction regards the first contention as a means of reaching the second and hopes to get the better of its opponents by abolishing all the landed proprietors and other privileged classes in order to set up on their ruins the empire of Liberty: in other words, that of outright democracy which these people suppose or, rather, are firmly convinced, will accompany the conquest. The other group hopes that precisely the contrary will happen: that is, that a vigorous government under the protection of the United States, together with a large emigration, will shortly deal a fatal blow to the last remnants of this corrupt and degraded society by restoring order and justice and nourishing the countless sources of prosperity and well-being that are stifled under our incapable hands. The first group goes so far as to flatter itself that the occupation of the capital by the Americans will be followed by the restoration of Farías's Government. In this single statement I am telling you more than I could on many a sheet of paper.

There is a third group, miserable and despised as are all middle-of-the-road groups. These individuals have no desire to encourage the prosecution of the war because they are convinced of our impotence. They are horrified by the calamities that the war is going to spread over our country and on this slothful and cowardly generation. But, on the other hand, these persons cannot make up their minds to stand by a peace settlement because they fear the disorder and upheaval that will ensue within the country, which will be destroyed by inflamed factions without honor, patriotism, or culture. They are aghast at the terrifying spectre of that immense accumulation of fragments of our army which yearn for peace so that they may devour the wretched remains of our dying civilization. These same fragments were the useless cowards who would not defend the honor and integrity of the Republic and who will become the fierce, bloodthirsty wolves that will swallow up whatever is left by the war and enslave the miserable survivors who will scarcely be able to stand upon their own feet. They, together with our pygmy politicians and traffickers in freedom, are creating as much consternation as the Yankees. And, therefore, just as a body pushed by two opposing and equal forces remains stationary, so remain those who, fearing everything from war, see nothing attractive in peace. Unhappily I am among this number, and I shall remain among them until a fresh and unexpected event causes the balance to tip one way or the other. When I was Minister I perhaps would have decided to throw my influence on the side of peace. Impelled by my duty as a private citizen, I shall not encourage a continuation of the conflict. But neither shall I oppose going on with the struggle, in so far as it affects my own circumstances, unless the foregoing suggestions for a settlement are carried out.

This, my friend, is the actual condition of the country such as I understand it, judging by the type of people that surround me. I present it to you in all its glaring truth so that you may form your own opinion. It is not known whether Scott has advanced, because he believes himself to be weak after his last victory and is awaiting the reinforcements that he has requested. He is wrong, since even with the handful of men that he has left he can occupy Mexico City without firing a shot. Here in the city the people consider themselves beaten and are resting their hopes on those states where they say there are still those who will save our national integrity. But I know those people rather well and I have no such hopes, understanding as I do that the heart of the Republic is Mexico City. Once this has been wounded, all the members of the body will perish.

Today's session came to a close after all kinds of blunders had been made. The first mistake was in neglecting to coordinate the constitutional reform measure with other agenda after this measure had been passed. The second was made when the decree against the Oaxaca authorities was passed by a majority of sixty-six to five! Such an exorbitant number of rascals is difficult to conceive of. In order to obtain this result it was necessary to struggle through a scandalous situation. The President ordered the attendants to lock the door of the Chamber and thus prevent the deputies from leaving. One enraged individual refused to let himself be ordered about and kicked the door down. At this the people in the gallery were thrown into an uproar and stopped the proceedings. Another deputy formally accused the Minister of War of issuing the order to restrict the freedom of the press under the Government's special powers. We really have one altar set up against another now. The Congress has made itself the object of universal hatred and contempt. If the famous decree of November 29[16] had not miscarried it would have been received now as a means of salvation. According to the present appearance of things the results of the Oaxaca affair may assume transcendental importance. It is not at all impossible that Baranda will resign, and he is the only man *qui pro hic et nunc*[17] can save the situation with the least disadvantage. Tonight there is to be a conference concerning the reshaping of the Cabinet as the first step in other, greater plans. In the midst of all these developments, who can tell where we are headed for if this reorganization does not take place?

In Jalisco events are in the making which will lead to a climax. These events will certainly not preserve our nationality but will rather produce dissension which perhaps will leave the Americans in peaceful possession of this important part of the Republic, from which they can easily subjugate the remainder. Our dreams of a federation are being transformed into a hideous nightmare for anyone who has a commanding view of the situation and who can at a glance see how the states are working. More common sense is being shown in San Hipolito, and the impartial, disinterested person is getting to the point where he doubts whether we are capable of forming a nation.

You are to keep to yourself the various bits of information contained in this letter, using them exclusively for your own guidance in the conduct of any transactions that you may engage in. And now that the devil has been tempting you to reveal confidences, I trust that you will not discuss

16 Probably Ramírez is referring here to the order given by Santa Anna on November 29, 1844, for the dissolution of the Congress, which was then very much opposed to him.
17 Who for the present.

these matters with the Governor, for he has done everything in his power to make me distrust him since his arrival there. I have not been able to understand why.

It is said that Scott has started a forward movement in the direction of S. A.'s forces. Franco will provide you with more details.

A new plot has been uncovered in the Bosom of Supreme Authority. It is intended to remove S. A. and render him incapable of action.

Goodbye.

(Signed)

Mexico City, May 12, 1847

Señor Don Francisco Elorriaga:

Baranda has finally resigned from the Cabinet, and, although the President has been reiterating all yesterday and today his determination to get him to take up his post again, I seriously doubt whether he will fall into the trap. I have absolutely no idea of what is going on, for I had, and still have, reasons to believe that the President was not entirely unaware of a certain political move that has been largely instrumental in bringing about Baranda's resignation. I suspect that something explosive lies behind all this, but I cannot say what it is or precisely where it will burst out. Up until today a plan has been on foot in the Congress to remove S. A., and in fact there has been some talk of taking away his extraordinary powers under the pretext that the constitution is no longer in force. It is not a remote possibility that Scott will appear in Mexico City at the very time when the Government finds that its hands are tied and that we are in the midst of the greatest disorder and confusion.

S. A. arrived in Puebla yesterday. He was not well received by the people there because they have no intention of offering resistance and are afraid that they will be forced to do so with S. A. in their midst. He has communicated with the Government, informing it in no uncertain language of his embarrassing predicament. He states that he may be attacked by Scott the day after tomorrow and cannot be sure of success. I fear that if he leaves the city the enemy will overtake him and cut him to pieces.

The Puebla Government, anticipating the wishes of the Yankees, had published a proclamation which is an exact copy of the one Taylor issued in the towns he has occupied. It referred to restricting the inhabitants to their homes, forbidding public prayers, etc. I do not know where all this will end.

Goodbye.

Mexico City, May 19, 1847

Señor Don Francisco Elorriaga

My dear friend:

I cannot tell you how much I regret the annoyances and embarrassment that the political change brought about in your state has obliged you to endure. I do not even entertain the hope that your situation may have improved, because I see that there is a *civil* party ready to encourage the ambitions of the *military* element, and here in Mexico City I find no sympathy for the new administration, nor a sufficiently powerful influence to create sympathy for it. I greatly fear that the promises made to the person who spoke on your behalf have remained only so many words and that his efforts cannot bring you any other help than the temporary assistance of the daily press. Nevertheless, you have nothing to fear with respect to yourself and your good name, for from the very first I have taken care to correct the false, contradictory statements that circulated, and I have no reason to fear for the future.

Great, very great, events have transpired these last three days, and as a result of them the seed of the Republic's future will be definitely planted.

On the night of the 17th a communication was received from S. A. to the effect that he was marching to this city. This announcement produced such consternation that on the following night everything was put in readiness for the issuance of a proclamation with the object of removing the General from the command of the army and from the Government of the Republic. Participating in this plan were the politicians who feared the establishment of a dictatorship under the extraordinary powers granted the Government, since the Congress was already considered dissolved. The advocates of peace and the property owners who feared the consequences of a siege strongly supported the plan. A third group composed of cowardly officers who had deserted from the army, together with many who harbored a grudge against S. A. and wanted to make one of my friends President, also backed the plan. Disagreement about a certain part of the plan, plus other considerations, helped out by the activity displayed by the Government, destroyed the contemplated revolution. As a result a committee was organized to confer with S. A. for the purpose of inducing him not to march to the capital and also for the purpose of divining his intentions. This committee was made up of Baranda, Trigueros, and myself. We did not sleep that night so that we could prepare for our journey, and we left yesterday at dawn.

We had not gone far from the city when we were convinced that we could not carry out our first purpose, because we met a host of sick and wounded men in the most wretched condition, and they informed us that the army was already on the march and was close to the city. Balked in our intentions, we thought of what we could do with S. A., or, rather, of what course of action we could persuade him to take. In the short time at my disposal it would be impossible for me to enter into details concerning the many grave situations we found ourselves in. But the enclosed paper will give you some idea of the most important facts. From it you will see the inconceivable state of self-denial and disinterestedness to which S. A. has been reduced. I drew up that document, which was read on five occasions and to which he subscribed of his own free will.[18] This frame of mind almost disappeared when that miserable Tornel suddenly came on the scene and inspired him with entirely different thoughts, beseeching him to march to the city and take over the Government, *because his own personal safety and the welfare of the Republic depended upon it.* Tornel assured him that only a handful of people were opposing him and that the entire city was clamoring for him. In spite of this S. A. did not change his mind, and, since the document was only in rough draft form, he insisted on having it clearly written out, whereupon he signed it. We then returned to the city, arriving about nine o'clock at night, positive that S. A. would not move from Ayotla until he received the Government's answer. The answer was being written down to the effect that he could return whenever he chose to do so, even to assume control of the Government, when one of his aides arrived with the information that he would be in the city within two hours. I do not know what his plans are, since I did not want to go out to receive him, although the carriage was waiting for us to take our reply to him and to explain the situation. The Cabinet members were largely to blame in this matter, for they did not want to manage the affair as it ought to have been managed, considering the fact that they had full authority to act. This weakness in the national character wherein we do not have nerve enough to give a definite "yes" or "no" has had its influence on the Government, impelling it to do what is most expedient and requires the least amount of reflection.

However, developments indicate only that there has been a mistake in judgment, not that the whole thing is past remedying. Nor do I believe that there has been a hostile attitude displayed up to now. My comments revolve only about this question of war, and when I discuss such matters I take into consideration only the circumstances that may contribute to its outcome. The Government has put an obstacle in its own path, for S. A.'s return brought about the completion of the new constitution with cries of "Finish the business" and a "Let us be going!" The deputies understand that the Government's powers will end with the death of the constitution. What will the Government do? We shall return to the old, hateful bickerings, and the Congress will either grant them [extraordinary powers] or refuse to do so, estimating these powers not by the magnitude of the necessity nor by the foreign enemy but by the greater or lesser degree of fear inspired by the person charged with exercising them. What a frightful predicament our country is in!

18 In the document Santa Anna said that, since the purpose of the revolution which was threatening was to oust him, he would serve the country by offering to resign both as President and Commander-in-Chief. Tornel's entreaties had their effect, however, and later the same day he sent another letter announcing that there were so many protests against his action that he was withdrawing his resignation. Callcott, *Santa Anna*, 263-64.

Private Correspondence
of the Minister of
Domestic and Foreign
Affairs

Mexico City, June 5, 1847[19]

Señor Don Francisco Elorriaga

My dear friend:

As you may have observed through the news reports, the stupendous variety or, rather, downright uncertainty of developments since my last letter to you had caused me to keep silent, since I was certainly unable to tell you anything that would have any possibility of being valid for twelve hours. Events followed one another like the waves of the ocean, now advancing, now receding. I am no more sure of the situation even today, but my silence cannot be prolonged further.

After countless intrigues pro and con that it would be impossible to enumerate, the present state of affairs finds the *puros,* considering themselves as out of the conflict, trying to make common cause with S. A. They believe him to be a beaten man, and by joining hunger with necessity they hope to produce abundance and a surplus. They are convinced that this alliance will put them on a footing firm enough to enable them to withstand their enemies. It seems that Tornel, the promoter of the new order and of the so-called freedom of his fellow men, will join the group.

In order to reach their goal they had to sacrifice several victims who by their fine capabilities and moral character would have stood in the way of their plans, and Baranda was the first victim. I would have been involved in all this if I had had any sort of pretensions; but since I do not ask anyone for favors and, therefore, require nothing from anyone, I have stood aside, seizing the first opportunity I could get to save one of my best friends. For three days I remained close to the President's offices so that I could prepare a way for Baranda that would lead him to an honorable resignation, and today the doors have been flung wide open for him. Tornel, Rejón, and other *puros* gathered around S. A. to convince him that the Ayotla occurrence was a plot that we had hatched in collusion with a certain political party in order to remove him from his command and thereby force him to renounce all his powers. They have also presented this latest resignation[20] as one prompted by the same motives. Although S. A. has indicated that he does not give credence to such trumped-up charges, he has profited by them in order to make sure of his future course of action. The rude blow that he has dealt Baranda today by annulling the decree of the

19 The text reads July 5, but this is either a misprint or an error by the author, as is made obvious in that section of the letter dealing with Baranda's resignation.
20 Baranda's.

17th of last month[21] *without even advising him beforehand or informing him about the matter afterward,* certainly makes it clear that he will not be stubborn in refusing Baranda's resignation. Acting upon these developments and taking advantage of such a fine opportunity, Baranda will send in his resignation tomorrow with merely a note attached and without going into further explanations. I also believe that he will refuse to give any explanation even if pressed for one, because he cannot possibly get another brilliant opportunity like this to leave with honor and respect.

The annullment of that law is one of the most infamous acts that I have ever seen, and one of the most infamous that could have taken place. Loathsome, pestilential filth has been pouring from the archiepiscopal mitre, infecting everything it touches. Irizarri has made an announcement in which he claims the right of immunity of *his church* (which is not that of Jesus Christ) in order to extort money from the working man and the tenant farmer. Loperena, that despicable liar, took advantage of this to negotiate with the Cabinet concerning the contribution of money which the Bishop of Michoacán was to make. The latter had been refusing to do this unless the law were repealed. S. A. consummated this useful trade by repealing the law in order to arrange for a purchase of muskets which Loperena is to provide at *fifteen pesos* apiece. I enclose a copy of the law. I am told that Rejón dictated it, and I suspect that this deal was intended to inflict a blow on Baranda and make it impossible for S. A. to check it.

Although in order to end so much rascality once and for all it would suffice to let matters take their course, one cannot be indifferent to the general chaos that will follow, or to the vengeance that will fall upon us. Therefore, there has been some discussion about putting an end to the situation by seeking a solution in the outlying districts. In fact, communications have been sent to the various states urging the legislatures to use their authority to declare the aforementioned law still in force in their respective territories. No one can prevent this, and the blow is sure to be effective. Will Durango do this? I have not dared to answer this question, because we are no longer what we once were, and I really do not know what we actually are.

In referring to this matter it strikes me that I ought to clear up the doubt you express in your last letter concerning the statements that might have caused me to believe that you were in sympathy with the change in the Durango administration. This is the statement from your letter of April 9: "Today we find ourselves with a new administration, and although there is nothing on which to base our feeling, as you realize, *we*

---

21 On May 17 Baranda issued a decree ordering that owners of urban and rural lands could not be asked for the payment or redemption of loans which they owed when the money had been borrowed from a corporation or pious funds. The action was taken because the clergy had been calling in its loans and converting its property into cash. This was a blow to agriculture and industry, both of which depended a great deal on church capital.

do have more and firmer hopes that affairs will go less badly, since the hatred and mistrust of the former administration could not have been greater than they were. *Now there will be more responsibility, and assuredly better order."* From this statement I presumed where your sympathies lay, because my convictions were diametrically opposed and it would seem that I was right. I have not confided my opinions in anyone, and what I have told you was based upon letters received from there.

Well, I have made up my mind and am settling my affairs so that I can go to Durango to share the bad times with you. At least for the first few days you will get away from it all by confining your attentions to your newly-arrived guest. I am already getting a good laugh when I think of all the guesses, opinions, etc., expressed by our profound politicians. I urge you to collect material with which we may amuse ourselves. I plan to leave on the 14th.

I am out of writing paper—
Goodbye.

Mexico City, August 11, 1847

Señor Don Francisco Elorriaga

My dear friend:

I did not write to you during the first days after my unhappy return to Mexico City because I was in a bad humor *and still am.* I did not write subsequent to that time because—yes, I shall tell you—because of sentiment and anger, since I believed that, sympathizing with my disappointment, you at least could have written me a few friendly words, just as I would expect from any other friend to whom I had given unmistakable testimony of my sincere esteem. I was completely mistaken, and even more so than I could foresee, because I did not even have a copy of the *Registro,* and only a few letters from my family. Your silence has not weighed heavily upon me, since I have thus found myself freed from all the torment of telling you about the countless *authentic* lies that were daily going the rounds and disappeared only to give way to others of the same kind. The Government has been the first to try out this system of deception. And I call it precisely that because the Government *knew* that the Americans would not come. Wearied by our confused political situation, they have at last started on the march, and the day before yesterday at two o'clock in the afternoon fired the fatal cannon shot that has, as it were, flung a pall of crepe over the city. Yesterday I spent a very dismal time watching the Victoria, Hidalgo, and Independencia battalions march by. They were for the most part composed of the flower of our young men. They have gone to take a stand at Peñón[22] and their introduction to war was hellish. A scorching hot morning and a cold, rainy night.

22 One of the principal fortified points for the defense of the capital located east of the city.

Yesterday considerable credence was being given to a rumor that a reconnoitering party of American troops had met with a reverse at the hands of Álvarez's men, but this rumor has not yet been confirmed. No one knows today where these troops are. You will die of shame and mortification— the reconnoitering party is composed of former prisoners in Puebla and it has already wiped out one of our guerrilla bands of a hundred men.

Our military chiefs generally believe that the Americans will advance to attack Peñón, the point where S. A. has intrenched with the largest force. Valencia has gone out with his division of 7,000 men to flank the Americans, marching around behind Texcoco, and Bravo, who is stationed at Mexical- zinco,[23] will cooperate. I very seriously doubt whether the enemy will fall into this trap in spite of his slow movements. I am afraid that he may turn and seize Tacubaya, or what would be still more ominous for us, pitch camp in some fortified place and there wait to be attacked. In the first case we would have to go out to meet him and risk success in an open battle. You know what the alternative would be in the second case. If he takes Tacu- baya, Mexico City will surrender in a few hours. It seems to me that the second move is more likely, perhaps because it is the one I fear most.

Our internal situation is very bad, much worse than you can imagine. And all because of the sluggishness of our leaders. It is costing the women great trouble to leave the city, although they ought to have been sent out before this. They are seizing upon everyone who happens to be bringing food into the city. If this goes on for any time there is no doubt as to what will happen. I propose to share the city's fate, for I must confess that my boredom has reached its height, and life no longer has any attractions for me. I doubt, too, whether I shall be running much risk.

In a packet of back numbers of the *Registro* I saw that the Congress and the President had given me the honor of suggesting me as a deputy in the future legislative body of Durango. I beg you to present my respects to my deputy friends and to the Governor. I have no doubt that there will be opposition to my election and I wish to make the best of this opportunity. Therefore, I *urge* you as my good friend not to take part in the election and I authorize this course of action so that you may dismiss from your mind any such idea, since I have firmly resolved not to take part in public affairs again. There was a time when I was so weak-minded as to think of seclusion as a sort of insult. You were equally weak, only in another sense. Today not even this feeling moves me, and the means are not important pro- vided I reach my goal. I have turned my ideas and labors in another di- rection and have become so immersed in them that not even the present violence can sway me in my purpose. I think that I am calm enough now to be able to go on, even in the midst of a bombardment.

I have not thought the circumstances propitious for dealing with your two problems, that of the excise tax and the other one that cannot be dis-

23 Texcoco is northeast of Mexico City. Mexicalzinco is a small town about five miles south of the capital.

cussed, but which is the one I shall not forget. You have been quite remiss about the first problem, for I asked you some time ago for the principal documents and delegated authority. Why have you not sent these? Why are you not sending them now?

Go to see the members of my family and calm their fears.

Goodbye.

(Signed)

Mexico City, August 11, 1847

Last-minute items:

They write from Peñón that they hope the coming attack will be the one that will decide our fate tomorrow or the day after. It still seems incredible to me that the Americans can have fallen into the trap set for them without making some daring effort to escape. Yesterday morning their advance columns reached Buenavista[24] and today they are probably in Ayotla. This is the military situation: S. A. is in Peñón with the largest force, Valencia with 5,000 men is in Texcoco, Álvarez with 3,000 horse is in contact with the enemy's rear guard, and Bravo holds Mexicalzinco with adequate forces. A reserve force has been left in Mexico City so as to be able to hasten to any point where it is needed. If the enemy does not withdraw in order to go around the lake by way of San Agustín,[25] he is certainly in a very bad predicament. If he does retreat, there will always be the chance of some major engagement. Álvarez's troops have already exchanged shots with the enemy's rear guard and have killed one soldier. The greatest enthusiasm has sprung up among our troops. God grant that this may continue!

The Governor of the important state of Mexico has refused the Government his artillery and troops, stating that he needs them to defend his state.

Mexico City, August 21, 1847

As was to be expected the Americans did not remain in the trap any longer than necessary for them to reconnoitre the situation. Proceeding around the lake, they unexpectedly appeared in San Agustín de las Cuevas where, either by accident or by intent, our experienced and expert generals were not waiting for them. Valencia, who was at Texcoco, executed a brilliant movement by placing his force in front of them before they reached that point. The day before yesterday the battle went on from one o'clock in the afternoon until nightfall, the enemy being unable to make him yield one inch of terrain, while they suffered considerable loss. S. A. went to his aid but kept at a distance, merely observing the action and not firing a shot. Then he retreated to San Angel with his division and sent Valencia a per-

24 Ayotla is approximately ten miles east of Peñón and Buenavista a short distance beyond Ayotla.

25 "The lake" refers to Lake Chalco which lay south of Ayotla and east of San Agustín. The latter was almost directly south of Mexico City and Mexicalzinco.

emptory order to abandon his position. The latter for very good reasons refused to obey. One of these reasons was the fact that the enemy had an open road to enable him to occupy Tacubaya, the key to Mexico City. In spite of this the order was repeated, with the additional command that if Valencia had to abandon all our supply trains and munitions to effect this move he was to do so. He again refused to obey, and thus the disagreement reached the point where Valencia informed S. A. that his conduct was that of a traitor and that he would not require his help. The next morning Valencia was surrounded by the enemy army that had profited by the darkness of night, and no one came to help him. S. A. started his division on the march when the fleeing troops caught up with him. Retreating without the semblance of order or plan, he was pursued by the Americans, who hacked his force to pieces without encountering any resistance. When he got to Churubusco two corps of national troops, the Independencia and the Bravos, came up to support those swaggering troops and held back the enemy at the bridge, causing some casualties in his ranks. But the burning of an artillery ammunition wagon, the command to retreat, and an enemy column which outflanked them determined the outcome of the struggle, and they were all taken prisoners along with their commanders, Anaya and Gorostiza. S. A. had previously given the order to abandon the fortified points and spike the guns, all of which facilitated the operations that decided our defeat. Everything, everything has been lost, except our honor. That was lost a long time ago. The generous foreign soldiers who composed the San Patricio companies perished in the struggle at the bridge, and the few who escaped were killed on the spot by their former comrades. Impartial eyewitnesses estimate our loss at 3,500 men, without counting the runaways who must have been in considerable number. The cavalry escaped with the smallest loss, as usually happens, because of its maneuverability and opportunities for retreat. Certain corps of blustering fellows refused to participate in the action.

You will, of course, suppose that no one can talk of anything but the horrible misfortune and that, to cap the climax, everybody, including the troops themselves, believes that S. A. betrayed us. I cannot bring myself to think this, because it is my firm conviction that the whole affair can be explained clearly as being the result of the incompetence and cowardice of our generals and our leaders who, with the exception of Valencia and some of those with him, have given proof of what they have been, are, and will continue to be: cowards, ignoramuses, and men wholly devoid of even one spark of personal honor. Judged by their ability they scarcely would make good sergeants. Judged by their character they are what one of our hapless poets has said of them:

> Tortoises in the country,
> Vultures in the city.

Select just one per cent of all of them to make an exception. And if you could see these men today, still walking along the avenues in droves with their wretched stars and medals gleaming on their breasts—and not one evidence of shame about them! A certain officer who escaped from the Churubusco affair assures me that at one fortified point all the troops retreated because their officers had not yet appeared. What will become of the people among whom such things occur? I am afraid that from this tremendous lesson we shall not derive even the one single, sad example that we ought to derive from it, and that no one will undertake to dispute our statement. You can probably guess what I mean.

Victoria and Hidalgo took no part in the struggle, and, sharing the general mood of the people, are refusing to lend aid.

Preparations to resist the enemy still continue, and there is still much blowing of bugles, marching and countermarching, as if we were going to defend ourselves *by the least costly means,* as the famous proclamation by the Minister of Foreign Affairs expresses it. But all this seems to me like so much sound and fury. A certain individual high in Government circles told me two hours ago that parleys which would probably lead to preliminary discussions about peace had already begun, as proved by the fact that the victorious army has not moved from its positions which today are those formerly held by us. This bit of news has been translated into our hypocritical, bombastic national tongue and states that the Americans have asked for an armistice in order to gather up their dead and wounded and that we have agreed to this so that we may do the same with our casualties. Ours are behind the enemy lines, three leagues from here. We are certainly incorrigible! An order has been issued forbidding the troops to discuss yesterday's events.

From my point of view it is all over. I foresaw this many months ago and, although I was grieved, I did all I could to avoid these needless misfortunes. I even got to the point where I could almost feel the very outcome itself, and then everything vanished as in a confused dream. Here there is a general lack of confidence, which is worse than even a lack of spirit. Spreading like an electric flame it has produced the resulting discouragement. On the other hand, I can assure you that there was once a general feeling of enthusiasm, and under other circumstances even the women would have fought. During the past few days I have not seen one person who evinced any fear. We were all prepared to sell our lives dearly, fighting at the parapets, in the event that our army suffered an ordinary defeat. Fear was spread among us by gold braid and military sashes, and I think it was only natural, for when the real test came these men realized either that they had made a mistake in their vocation or that they were completely unaware of what their uniforms required of them.

In spite of all this, I am not overwhelmed by the present state of affairs, since the disappointments of war are by their very nature transitory. What frightens me is the future. I cannot even guess what will become of us. I do not think it beyond possibility that the remnants of our troops may fight on the side of the Americans. You will see when and how this may come to pass.

Tell the members of my family that I am safe and in good health. But my heart is broken.

(Signed)

Mexico City, August 25, 1847

What I told you has turned out to be true. The armistice was declared today, and the peace treaty, or at least the preliminaries to it, will follow. Pedraza, Lacunza, and Antonio Garay were named to the commission which was to conclude the peace. The first excused himself and today must have left the town where he had been staying. The second is in Toluca and certainly will not come. If events move with this sort of alacrity, who knows how long our intolerable situation will continue, a situation that is especially horrible for all the unhappy towns occupied by the Yankees? They have sacked most of the towns, and their commander either cannot or does not wish to restrain them.

An effort was made to reconvene the Congress but to no avail. Eight or more deputies who were in Toluca came out with this suggestion: that all those deputies living here or elsewhere assemble outside the city. The idea does not seem to me to be either legal or proper. But their object had to correspond with their principles and methods. This is why I thought that the Congress had been dissolved at an opportune time. I wanted to avoid this occasion for shame, in addition to other reasons. They say that the place of the Congress will be taken by a Council of Notables. But if they are thinking of anything more than keeping up appearances, the idea seems to me to be as foolish as it is impractical.

Valencia has risen in revolt at Toluca, but in a *cautious, peaceful* manner. That is to say, he has about 1,400 men in barracks and is getting new recruits without enunciating any definite program of action. In a fiery speech to his troops he did reveal the program that he is credited with having formulated, proclaiming a fight to the death against the Americans and his determination to have S. A. beheaded.

The vagueness that you will probably note in the first lines dealing with Salas can be explained by what I have said in my previous communication.

An order has been issued for the arrest of all the officers who fought under Valencia. This seems to me to be an atrociously unjust and impolitic procedure.

Several mail deliveries have come in, and I have not yet received any word from you. If we are going to continue on the *blow for blow* basis, my letters will soon stop, once and for all.

Goodbye.

(Signed)

Mexico City, September 11, 1847

My dear friend:

In the last mail I scarcely had time to write a few words to Don Germán. This was because I had been misinformed by the couriers themselves. Taking for granted that you know what I wrote him, I shall tell you that although the news was received in the midst of much turmoil, it turned out to be accurate, with the exception of a few details. The important part is that we undoubtedly would have won a complete, outstanding victory if the cavalry had charged as it was commanded to,[26] but the cowardly officers did not obey any of the five orders given them. Andrade, Brito, and the rest did the same thing they had done at Padierna in the action on the 19th. Simeón Ramírez refused to go to the aid of Pérez, and the latter had to retreat from Casa Mata with 1,200 men, losing the position and an entire battalion which was routed. Prior to that the cavalry had turned the whole thing into a fiasco, exposing our troops to a complete rout by not occupying at four o'clock in the morning a magnificent hill on which it could have cut the enemy to pieces. General Santa Anna, relying on this maneuver, discovered that the cavalry did not appear on the field until a quarter of six and from the opposite direction. By this time everything was over.

Quite different was the scene at Molino del Rey, which is behind Chapúltepec Forest. It was defended by *national* troops under the command of the valiant but luckless León and Valderas. A dense column of troops attacked them with great courage, driving them out at the point of the bayonet. Our men reformed their ranks and, making a bayonet charge, recovered the position, forcing the enemy to run like a streak of lightning. Then the enemy charged again and gained the position once more, only to be dislodged a second time by our troops. And thus a fearful carnage ensued in which the struggle went on, hand-to-hand, costing the lives of the two valiant officers. Meanwhile the miserable, cowardly cavalry remained where it was, watching that scene which it could have changed for our honor and advantage, saving the lives of two brave men who were worth infinitely more than all of them put together. General Álvarez, in despair over the vile cowardice of his disobedient companions, took several soldiers who had volunteered to go with him, and, acting as a plain captain, made an attack which came too late but which finally saved five of the ten guns that had been taken from us. At eleven o'clock the enemy made another more formidable attack on Chapúltepec Castle, penetrating to the Forest. But there they were hurled back with great loss. This was their last attempt. The cavalry continued its inactivity, and from this fact and a favorite saying of Andrade's, in which he declares that in all the latest fighting he has been placed on terrain on which he *cannot maneuver*, the public has coined a pungent epigram that characterizes the cavalry. They say that

26 Ramírez is referring to the battle of Molino del Rey, a mill which was a mile north of Tacubaya and about one-half mile west of Chapúltepec. Casa Mata was a stone edifice just a very short distance west of Molino del Rey.

our cavalry *is suffering from the cholic*. Shortly before noon a skillfully aimed grenade or bomb from the Castle set fire to Casa Mata, where the Americans had placed a large number of field pieces. It blew up with a terrific explosion, killing about a hundred of their men. The enemy started to withdraw about one o'clock, and at two o'clock had left the field completely.

Of course you understand that the casualty figures are almost irreconcilable. But relying upon the sober calculations of General Bravo, which are confirmed by reliable persons who visited the scene of the struggle and who later received news from Tacubaya, we estimate that the enemy's losses totaled at least 1,000 men while ours were 600, both sides having reason to mourn over their sizable casualties. There has been a great deal of talk these past few days about the death of Worth.[27] Haro, referring to the President's testimony, told me the same thing. But yesterday General Vizcaino, who came from our camp, told me that he had learned from a captured American officer that General Pillow was the officer killed, although he did not deny that Worth might have been wounded. Letters received from Tacubaya last night maintain that among the superior officers twenty-seven were casualties and twenty of these had died already. It is said that among these was Scott's nephew, a colonel, but other people say that they have seen documents signed by him after the battle.

The fact that this was a severe battle of some consequence is indicated by two singular developments in the enemy's tactics. In the first place, up to the present moment (nine o'clock in the morning) he has not repeated his attack but is taking a stand along the line formed by the highways from San Borja to San Antonio Abad[28] and has confined himself to unimportant skirmishes. Secondly, quite a few of his troops have become stragglers and deserters. Yesterday morning a body of his cavalry advanced along one of the highways but retired after a couple of shots from our battery. In the afternoon some of his cavalry again advanced although they kept out of range. Everyone thought that the battle would be continued early this morning, but all this silence and lack of activity are, to tell the truth, causing me perhaps more alarm than the din of conflict. I fear a surprise or some other kind of unexpected development. The city presents an imposing aspect that becomes terrible at times. The church bells, which have been silent for many days, ring only to spread the alarm; and this sound of alarm bells, which produces feverish excitement in the streets and public squares, is followed by the silence of desolation, because half the inhabitants crowd the rooftops to see what their fate may be, while the other half lock themselves indoors or rush to arms to prepare to defend themselves to the last. On the 8th there was constant excitement, with a ringing of bells that became unbearable, and yesterday this ringing, ordered by that silly, pre-

27   Spelled "Word" in the text.
28   South of Mexico City.

tentious fellow, Tornel, filled the entire city with terror, causing some people to go about shouting that the enemy was already in the city.

This situation naturally prompts me to tell you what I think about one of the points you refer to in your letter. I mean the disturbing question concerning the Congress of the state of Mexico, which must have made a decided impression upon you. You realize that the Congress is made up of rascals and quarrelsome individuals, and, although the state of Mexico is the first in the federation, it is governed by *a madman*. I am not using this term as an epithet, but as one that clearly expresses my convictions. I do indeed believe that he has taken leave of his senses and that his insanity is the result of his ambition, which is not the innocent sort but one inspired by evil intentions. The chronicle of Olaguível's activities is endless and is an inexhaustible source of entertainment for all classes of society. In his political-diplomatic-military farce he brings together and discusses over and over again all kinds of matters, except those of real significance, and still his colleagues in the Congress *keep their friendship* with him. There was a time when, owing to my sympathies with S. A., I might have hesitated to make such an accusation. But now this accusation, although perhaps based upon a misconception, must be considered the true expression of my opinions. Zacatecas's conduct does not surprise me, for in it I can perceive the confirmation of an old, despised political maxim: *individuals, rather than political systems, produce the happiness of peoples and bring honor to nations*. The state of Mexico of today and the Zacatecas of yesteryear could have exchanged their reputations by making an exchange of governors.

I am not surprised that I have been considered as a candidate for Governor, however extraordinary this may seem, for ever since 1835, when I assumed my duties as a secretary in the Government amid bullets fired by a tumultuous crowd, until 1844, when I became the Commanding General, I have had plenty of opportunities to accustom myself to this kind of attention. Do not for one moment suppose, however, that I have received the suggestion badly. If formerly or at the present time I considered that the public offices entrusted to me, and which I have found to be more burdensome than lucrative, were given me simply out of charity or because they were superfluous, I would have flung them back in the faces of those who gave them to me; for you know well enough that I have never sought any kind of office, nor anything else. Thank God, I have enough to keep me from requiring anything from anybody. No, I have calmly watched the development of events, and if many times I was unable to show gratitude I was always embarrassed because of it. I was always accorded a signal honor by being unfairly given the hard, jagged bones that no one else wanted to gnaw. You have also noted that I have tried to break them without seeking to get the marrow and that I have had enough generosity not to spoil someone else's pleasure by bitter reproaches. Perhaps this is the first time that I have spoken seriously about this matter, although not in this precise sense but solely to maintain in your sight the good reputation you impute to me. I would feel sorry indeed if you were to think that I believed I would be called to the job by the freely offered, spontaneous votes of my constituents. On the other hand, I have reason to think that I am being considered because of the urgent situation, but I am regarded as a last resort—someone who would be ignored under less threatening circumstances and as long as there was hope of any other solution. In spite of these convictions, far from being offended I feel more than humble; I am grateful. Although someone else might perhaps consider this an opportune occasion to make compensation for several years of bitter difficulties by a mere refusal, I can say that I have forgotten all these past troubles.

You know that I am too frank to say what I do not really feel. And I can also understand that I am speaking to my *alter ego,* for it would not be very honest and generous of me not to let these sincere expressions from the bottom of my heart reach the ears of those who have already made a great sacrifice in simply thinking of me, not to say working actively in my behalf. My only wish is that those who are far away understand that I am cognizant of what is transpiring.

Although the persons who have put themselves at the head of this move enjoy enough influence to augur success, they ought to realize that they will have to deal with strong resistance. With this in mind I have tried to anticipate the possibility of their reflecting upon this exigency, because it would be quite embarrassing for me to see that after so much trouble on their part the whole attempt had produced only failure. If you people in Durango, under the spell of our routine system of politics, are thinking only of escaping from the present evil and of winning the election without looking ahead, you are making a mistake. Are those gentlemen sufficiently acquainted with my ideas, and for this reason have they made up their minds to support my candidacy? Permit me to doubt this. And in the event that I am mistaken, see that they alter their opinions by taking a look at the following program, which I would carry out if I were made Governor.

A great economy in expenses and the distribution of public revenues; the strictest supervision in collection and use; prompt and efficient performance of their duties by the servants of the state, although always in proportion to compensation; all requisite energy to carry out the laws without, of course, falling into arbitrary policies. To sum up: to attain what constitutes the life and the soul of society, namely, to consolidate the elements of morality and public order by raising a prudent but firm hand against abuses so that they may be eradicated. As a result, I shall not ignore my duties in order to make friends, nor shall I remember that I have had opponents in the past. Although it may be necessary for me to show some consideration here and there, since the staff of the Governor is not made of steel nor is excessive severity the way to reform a vicious society, I shall not, on the other hand, make this the basis of my conduct but rather the exception. If it came to a question of serious misconduct I would have no pity, not even upon my own family. Finally, I would be zealous in preserving the authority and dignity of my office, and in this respect I would tolerate absolutely nothing that would tend to lessen it, unless an irresistible force, or even greater evils, forced me to do so. Nevertheless, in defending the dignity of my office, as I assure you I mean to defend it, I would give little thought to the mere *possession* of that office, because I look upon it not as a favor to me but as a responsibility. Every time the discussion was about me personally, I would act in my capacity of Governor as I acted in that of Minister of Foreign Affairs. I would also want to have the widest latitude in carrying to completion all important business that requires complete unity of plan and action, whether in originating new programs or simply in reforming old ones. I would want this freedom of action because constant experience has proved to me that legislative bodies are entirely undependable in getting such things done. Now, I would not be too exacting with respect to this matter, since the responsibility and the blame would not fall upon my shoulders. I presume you will do me the justice of believing that when I speak about the reform of abuses, etc., I do not intend to enter the lists against the clergy or any other group, as some people might imagine I would do, to judge from the stupid, vulgar criticism and even gross slanders that have been hurled at me. But my well established reputation for being an aristocrat ought to have convinced many of my critics that that characteristic was incompatible with class hatred.

Once my ideas have become known and I have given you authority, or rather my friendly permission, to communicate them to the people who have chosen me as their candidate, you as a public official and as my true friend, will discuss these ideas in detail so that if there is anything in them to surprise people or to prevent them from supporting me wholeheartedly, they can select another candidate. These are not conditions that I am imposing upon you, but actual facts that I am acquainting you with, so that you may not be caught by surprise. That is why I have hastened to explain them, hoping thereby that my remarks may reach you in time to remedy any mistake that may be made. The matter is of the utmost consequence and of a nature that demands complete loyalty and frankness. I cannot promise you anything in the spirit of one who deals in flattery, because I do not know what I shall be able to do. I also make no promise because such a promise would sound like an impertinent claim.

But if it is no longer possible for you people to retrace your steps, there is yet no reason why you should feel disturbed about it. Even if this entire program of mine is accepted in every particular, I still have one more condition to stipulate. And this one is really a condition. You know better than I that the unhappy people there are being menaced by an insidious, fatal cancer that can be destroyed only by a remedy from Mexico City. By "remedy" I mean that the Governor must be free to carry on his duties. At least the impediments which up to the present time have hindered and nullified his efforts must be removed. Therefore, if I did not get assurance of this, I would not accept the Governorship. As far as I am concerned, jobs with a mere tinsel glitter have no appeal for me. I have too much pride to assume the role of comic King. Acting upon what I have just said and ignoring in my remarks anything that might cause you embarrassment, you will please inform your friends there to act accordingly. They are to be advised that, far from regretting any change they may make, I shall be deeply grateful and shall deem it a fine gesture, one that will be a true response to my frankness.

I was about to continue this, but the ringing of alarm bells in the Cathedral warns us of an attack by the enemy. It is three o'clock in the afternoon. God help us! A few moments ago I was frightened and horrified by news of the terrible slaughter of our luckless Irish soldiers who fell into the enemy's hands. I call this an atrocious act, because Scott had promised to free them, giving this promise at the request of some ladies from Mexico City who had taken refuge in Tacubaya. The English Minister had also made representations. I shall continue with an account of the day.

We have been attacked at three points simultaneously: at Chapúltepec, along the Piedad Highway and the Niño Perdido Highway. One of these attacks is bound to be a mere feint, and our success depends upon finding out which one it is.

Quarter after four. The troops approaching Chapúltepec were fired on five times and withdrew without replying. The American battery is keeping up an incessant fire on the intrenchments on Niño Perdido Highway, but the fire is not being returned. Three badly aimed bombs have been fired at us.

Seven o'clock. The cannonading has been diminishing since five o'clock but it still continues. An action begun so late may turn into a surprise attack during the night, unless the enemy has made up his mind to keep our troops under a continuous strain, hoping for some careless maneuver on their part.

Nine o'clock has just struck, and nothing new has developed. I shall make haste to finish this letter lest something happen to prevent me from mailing it.

Tell all the members of my family that everything is about the same here and be sure and keep Don Germán posted on the news I send you.

Goodbye.

Mexico City, September 30, 1847

My dear friend:

I have not received any word from you to which I can reply, because, since the unfortunate inhabitants of this city are being treated as enemies, there has been no opportunity to get mail in from the outside. Where it is being held heaven only knows. We have hopes that the mail will eventually be permitted to come in, and then I shall know what I have to reply to.

What shall I tell you? Well, to be frank, nothing, because this city is no longer the center of political life. According to reports, the center has been transferred to many other centers that will exhaust whatever political life is left to us by our enemy who is oppressing and humiliating us. How I would like to bring home this lesson to certain politicians who have talked incessantly about despotism, etc.! Here they would see and get a taste of what it means to live *without guarantees!* It is all so frightful. I must say that those who have conquered us, brutally savage as they are, have conducted themselves in a manner different from that of European armies belonging to nations that bear the standard of civilization. This does not mean that they do not commit countless excesses every day. But we have here a phenomenon consisting of mingled barbarism and restraint. This has been the situation for several days, and there is no way to account for it.

Open fighting ceased the third day after the city was occupied; but the undercover struggle goes on, and it is assuming a fearful aspect. The enemy's forces are growing weaker day by day because of assassinations, and it is impossible to discover who the assassins are. Anyone who takes a walk through the streets or goes a short distance away from the center of the city is a dead man. I have been told that a small cemetery has been found in a pulque tavern where deadly liquor was dispensed for the purpose of assuring an increasing number of victims. Seven corpses were discovered inside the establishment, but the tavern keeper could not be found. I am also told that the number of those who have been taken off this way amounts to 300, without counting those dying of sickness and wounds. Five days ago a funeral cortege with the bodies of four officers passed by my residence. The plague has begun to show its signs, and the monuments that those filthy soldiers have scattered along the streets of their quarters unmistakably testify to the fact that dysentery is destroying them. I have never before seen such sodden drunkenness, nor any more scandalous or impudent than the drunkenness that holds these men in its grip. Nor have I ever seen more unrestrained appetites. Every hour of the day, except during the evenings, when they are all drunk, one can find them eating everything they see.

The Palace and almost all public buildings have been savagely ransacked and destroyed. I think it only right to say, however, that our disgraceful rabble were the ones who began it all. When the enemy's troops entered the Palace, the doors had already been broken down and the building had been plundered. Three days later the embroidered velvet canopy was sold for *four pesos* at the Palace entrance. The Government records and other items were sold for two reales. The infamous and eternally accursed Santa Anna abandoned us all, both individuals and property, to the mercy of the enemy and did not leave even one sentinel to defend us.

In Durango you probably know more of what is going on than I do, and you no doubt can see how horrible our future is. I am forwarding to you some documents, two of which I want you to keep as testimony of the iniquitous and shameful rule that the Americans have imposed upon us. The sad thing about all this is that the punishment has been deserved.

Forward the enclosed letters and tell the members of my family that we are all in good health. Do not forget your friend, who holds you in great esteem.

(Signed)

INDEX

Alamán, Lucas, 63, 68, 73-75.
Almonte, Juan N., relations with Paredes, 15-16, 20, 26-27, 32, 34-36, 39-40, 50-54, 57-63; relations with Santa Anna, 69-74, 79, 83, 85, 90, 110, 115.
Álvarez, Juan, 134, 150-151, 155.
Amigo del Pueblo, 49, 60.
Ampudia, Pedro, 41, 43, 76.
Anaya, Pedro María, replaces Gómez Farías, 110-112, 123, 129, 133, 136-137, 141, 144; Secretary of War under Herrera, 11, 13-14.
Archbishop of Mexico, 26, 45, 63, 106-107, 148.
Army, Mexican, defense of Mexico City, 149-157, 160; retreat in the east, 118-124, 128, 132-141, 144; under Herrera, 24-27, 29-36, 41, 43; under Paredes, 51-54, 61, 66-67; under Santa Anna, 78, 81, 89-91, 101, 116.
Army's General Manifesto, 53-54.

Bankhead, Charles, 129.
Baño de las delicias affair, 29.
Baranda, Manuel, 60, 71-72, 75, 77, 79-81, 90, 111-112, 115-116, 123-129, 131-148.
Bases Orgánicas, 35, 39.
Batista Morales, Juan, 47.
Bravo, Nicolás, defense of Mexico City, 150-151, 156; relations with Paredes, 12, 15-16, 26, 54, 57, 63; relations with Santa Anna, 135, 138.
Brokers, power in Mexican congress, 17-22.
Bustamante, Anastasio, reaction to Paredes revolt, 12, 17, 26-30, 33, 36, 54; relations with Santa Anna, 135.

Canalizo, Valentín, 18, 118, 121.
Carmelites, 41.
Centralism, 53-56.
Cerro Gordo, battle of, 118-121, 128, 134, 139.
Chamber of Deputies, actions during attack on Mexico City, 154; and Otero, 46-48, 119, 127, 129-133; debates in spring and summer of 1847 on cabinet's relation to congress, 129-133, 136-137, 140-144, on carrying on the war, 120-123, 125-131, 140-141; on constitutional reform, 119, 127, 131, 133, 136, 138, 140, 143; on Oaxaca affair, 129-133, 140, 143; election of president and vice-president, 92-95; on British mediation, 116, 122, 131, 140; reaction to law of January, 1847, 104-105, 112-113; reaction to Paredes revolt, 13-23, 33; under Santa Anna and Gómez Farías, 87-91.
Chapúltepec, 33, 155, 160.
Church, economic position in spring and summer, 1847, 123-124, 148;

forced loan, 93; properties and privileges, 75-76, 81, 91; reaction to law of January, 1847, 98-100, 105-106, 112-113; reaction to revolt against Gómez Farías, 105-108.
Churubusco, 152-153.
Ciudadela, Mexico City, 24, 30, 32-36, 41, 43, 45, 69.
Congress, see Chamber of Deputies.
Constitution, attempt at constitutional reform, 1847, 119, 127, 129, 130-131, 136, 140, 143; of Paredes, 53-56; of 1824, 12, 23; reinstatement of constitution of 1824, 69, 71.
Corruption in government, 25, 55-58, 60, 62, 64, 90, 130.
Cortina, José G. de la, 54.
Councils, 51, 56-58, 62-63, 80-84, 93.
Couto, Bernardo, 18-21, 28, 33, 44.
Cuevas, Luis, 11, 19, 22, 33.
Cumplido, Ignacio, 47, 64.

Decembrists, 71, 82, 91.
Diario Oficial, 11, 19, 44, 68, 85.
Don Simplicio, 83, 106, 127.
Durango, 58-59, 71, 74, 88-89, 95-96, 101-102, 139, 148-150, 157-159.

Echevarría, Pedro, 48.
Elorriaga, Francisco, candidate for president and vice-president, 93-96; letters from Ramírez, 68-161; Ramírez's advice to, 74, 82, 84-91, 95-99, 144-145, 158-159.
England, mediation proposals, 116, 122, 129-131, 140.
Esnaurrizar, Antonio, 57, 61-62.

Farías, see Gómez Farías.
Federalism, 19, 23, 28, 38.
Federalist Society, 75.
Federalists, alliance with Santa Anna, 68, 71; ideas in 1846, 75-79, 82; internal quarrels, 85-86, 90; reaction to Herrera's government, 25-26, 44.
Filisola, Vicente, 54, 89.
Finances, lack of under Herrera, 17-22, 29; under Paredes, 57-58, 61; under Santa Anna, 78, 81, 88-93, 98-101, 105, 112-113, 119-124, 127-128, 134, 139-140, 148.
Fourth Battalion, 22, 30, 36, 53.

Garay, Antonio, 26, 154.
Gómez Farías, Valentín, election as vice-president, 90, 94; establishment of government of Santa Anna, 77-82; forced out of office, 109-112; position after passage of law of January, 1847, 99-107; revolt against Paredes and return of Santa Anna, 67-73; spokesman for the federalist faction, 12-13, 39, 63; trouble with moderados, 86-87.